Working and Breastfeeding Made Simple

Nancy Mohrbacher, IBCLC, FILCA

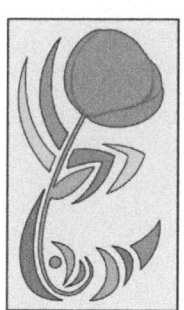

Praeclarus Press, LLC

www.PraeclarusPress.com

D0907941

Praeclarus Press, LLC
2504 Sweetgum Lane
Amarillo, Texas 79124 USA
806-367-9950
www.PraeclarusPress.com

DISCLAIMER
The information contained in this publication is advisory only
and is not intended to replace sound clinical judgment or individ-
ualized patient care. The author disclaims all warranties, whether
expressed or implied, including any warranty as the quality, ac-
curacy, safety, or suitability of this information for any particular
purpose.

ISBN: 978-1-9398071-3-7

Cover Design: Ken Tackett
Acquisition & Development: Kathleen Kendall-Tackett
Copy Editing: Diana Cassar-Uhl, Chris Tackett
Layout & Design: Todd Rollison
Operations: Scott Sherwood

Table of Contents

Foreword

Every day I get questions from employed and soon-to-be employed mothers about preparing to return to work, maintaining milk supply, and fitting breastfeeding into their work routines. Two of the most popular articles at Kelly-Mom.com address concerns about the amount of expressed milk baby needs and how mom can increase her pumping amounts.

If you're returning to work after having a baby, you probably have many of these same questions:

"My baby is due soon and I'm planning to breastfeed. I only have six weeks of maternity leave. What do I need to do to prepare to return to work and continue breastfeeding? Which breast pump should I get? How can I talk to my employer and co-workers about pumping? Any tips on finding a breastfeeding friendly child care provider?"

"My baby is 10 weeks old and I return to work in two weeks. I'm having a hard time finding the time and a place to pump. My baby has also been refusing to take a bottle for the last week, and my job isn't flexible enough to let me leave to feed her."

"My baby is 4 months old. I work full-time, and pump every three hours. My baby is drinking more milk than I can pump. How can I increase the amount of milk I'm pumping?"

"I started a new job one month ago and pumping is very difficult. I would like to wean my older baby to formula and solids during the day, with breastfeeding when we are together. How can I make this work?"

"I need to start traveling three to four days per week for my job. My baby is 6 months old. How do I maintain my breastfeeding relationship despite multi-day separations?"

According to the U.S. Bureau of Labor Statistics, more than half of mothers with children under the age of one are employed. As a result, many women in the United States who are planning to breastfeed during the first year need reliable information on maintaining breastfeeding when mother and baby are separated. This book is for these mothers.

Working and breastfeeding is *not* a simple thing for many mothers, especially in the beginning. With her years of experience helping employed mothers, Nancy simplifies the subject, focusing on how breastfeeding works. She will help you look at your individual needs and goals, and customize a plan to make the most of breastfeeding in your individual situation. This book will help you make the most of your time before you return to work, organize your return to work, and understand how milk production works, so you can make milk expression and breastfeeding work.

For the past 15 years, I have kept Nancy's books on my desk, and this book will definitely get a spot among the rest. It is well-referenced, well-organized, and answers the questions that mothers are asking about working and breastfeeding. There are also many additional resources given, including relevant websites, videos, and handouts.

There is nothing like the joy of seeing your baby smile as you return to him, and snuggle in to enjoy a relaxing feed. Breastfeeding helps you stay connected to your baby while you are apart, and re-connect when you are back together. *Working and Breastfeeding Made Simple* will help you to maintain this connection and meet your breastfeeding goals.

Kelly Bonyata, BS, IBCLC
KellyMom.com
St. Petersburg, Florida

Introduction

If you're reading this, chances are you are planning (or have already begun) to work and breastfeed. Why do you need this book? First, you'll find tips and insights that can simplify your life and make the process less confusing. Second, despite the glut of internet information and major breastfeeding-promotion efforts, without some inside knowledge, you're unlikely to meet your breastfeeding goals. I chose this book's content to help you avoid the experience of most women. A 2012 study found that two thirds of American mothers who wanted to exclusively breastfeed for three months didn't (Perrine, Scanlon, Li, Odom, & Grummer-Strawn, 2012).

Employed mothers—especially those working full time—are even less likely to reach their breastfeeding targets than other mothers (Ogbuanu, Glover, Probst, Hussey, & Liu, 2011). In every developed country around the world, breastfeeding rates drop quickly after birth. Even in areas where new mothers receive many months of paid maternity leave, such as the U.K., breastfeeding rates plummet during the early weeks. But before I say more about the challenges and how this book can help you avoid and overcome them, I'd like to share with you the latest on why breastfeeding matters so much to you and your baby.

Why Breastfeeding Matters

Most mothers know that babies who are not breastfed are at greater risk for many health problems. But only recently have we begun to understand the risk to mothers when breastfeeding is cut short. Breastfeeding is not just important to your baby. It's also important to you.

Breastfeeding and You

Breastfeeding is a key women's health issue. A growing body of research has linked a lack of breastfeeding and early weaning to the number one killer of women, heart disease, as well as breast and ovarian cancers, metabolic syndrome, type 2 diabetes, and many other serious health problems. Breastfeeding even affects your response to stress (helping you cope with it better), your resistance to illness (boosting it), and how well and how long you sleep (longer and deeper).

For years, people assumed that breastfeeding was draining to mothers. While fatigue is a normal part of life for all new parents, it turns out this assumption was dead wrong. Your body adapts to lactation by reducing the energy required to make milk, which also improves your other body functions. Scientists think that milk-making actually "primes" or "resets" your metabolism after birth to boost your metabolic efficiency (Stuebe & Rich-Edwards, 2009). Lactation improves digestion and increases absorption of nutrients (Hammond, 1997). It increases your sensitivity to the hormone insulin in the short and long term. For every year you breastfeed, over the next 15 years, your risk of developing type 2 diabetes decreases by about 15% (Stuebe, Rich-Edwards, Willett, Manson, & Michels, 2005).

Breastfeeding and Your Baby

Thousands of studies have reported on the health drawbacks when babies are not breastfed. The American Academy of Pediatrics 2012 Policy Statement recommends exclusive breastfeeding for the first six months and a minimum of one year of total breastfeeding (AAP, 2012). Babies who are *not breastfed* are at increased risk of the health problems.

- 257% increased risk of lower respiratory infections

- 170% increased risk of upper respiratory infections

- 100% increased risk of ear infections

- 67% increased risk of asthma

- 72% increased risk of allergic rashes

- 178% increased risk of digestive tract infections

- 41% increased risk of type 1 diabetes

- 56% increased risk of Sudden Infant Death Syndrome

But a healthier first year is not the end of the story. One compelling reason that one year of breastfeeding is recommended is that these health differences are not restricted to infancy. Babies who do not breastfeed or who wean early are more likely to develop the following conditions as they mature: obesity, diabetes, inflammatory bowel diseases, celiac disease, and childhood leukemia and lymphoma. For an overview of why breastfeeding matters from a health standpoint to both you and your baby, see the 2010 article "The Risks and Benefits of Infant Feeding Practices for Women and Their Children" (Stuebe & Schwarz, 2010): *http://www.ncbi.nlm.nih.gov/pmc/articles/PMC2812877/pdf/ RIOG002004_0222.pdf.*

You may find this information disturbing or motivating, but in either case, you need it. In order to make a truly informed decisions, parents need to know how breastfeeding impacts lifelong health. When it comes to breastfeeding, knowledge is definitely power. Knowing what's at stake may help you get through the rough spots that many breastfeeding mothers experience.

For many women, though, the importance of breastfeeding to health isn't even on their radar. Breastfeeding's main appeal is that it increases the connection between mother and baby. When you and your baby are regularly apart, your emotional connection with your baby looms large, as Marge describes.

I loved that this was something only I could do for my baby. I was worried he would think his nanny was his mom, but everyone reassured me children always know who the mom is—from the intensity of the relationship and connection. Still, the breastfeeding and providing all his milk made me feel connected, a 24/7 mom.

—*Marge G., Ohio, USA*

How can you make breastfeeding—and the close connection that it fosters—a reality? That's what this book is about.

Let Me Be Your Guide

My love for breastfeeding began when I breastfed my own three sons, who are now grown. I started working with mothers as a volunteer in 1982. After I became board-certified, for 10 years, I ran a large private lactation practice in the Chicago area, where I worked one-on-one with thousands of families. I also worked for eight years as a lactation consultant for a major breast pump company, educating health care providers and answering mothers' questions about milk supply and how to make the most of a breast pump. I wrote breastfeeding books used worldwide by parents and professionals, which has kept me current in the lactation research. When I began writing this book, I worked in a corporate lactation program, where I talked daily to women who were pregnant, on maternity leave, and who had returned to work. As you can probably tell, I have a passion for helping breastfeeding mothers. I'd love to share what I've learned with you.

In this book, I've included the key ingredients that make breastfeeding work. It's not complicated. In fact, much of it is very simple. But without this information, working and breastfeeding may be more difficult or more worrisome than it needs to be. These pages include the latest on many of the burning issues you may face: milk production, maternity leave, pumping, flexible job options, childcare, milk storage and handling, work-life balance, and much, much more.

But before we get into these specifics, let me circle back to the sobering figures I mentioned in the beginning on how many women wean earlier than intended. I'd like to explain some of the dynamics that affect these numbers.

The Challenges in Brief

Why is breastfeeding so challenging for so many mothers? One reason is that many mothers and babies don't get the help they need from the institutions that touch their lives. For example, the U.S. Centers for Disease Control and Prevention report that after birth, one in every four U.S. newborns is supplemented in the hospital with infant formula (Centers for Disease Control and Prevention, 2012). Giving newborns formula unnecessarily is a common first step to milk-production problems. Science tells us that worry about milk production is the number one reason women wean before they'd planned. Because many health professionals receive no breastfeeding training, they often give mothers conflicting advice while they are still in the hospital. And some of this advice undermines mothers' best efforts to breastfeed.

After mother and baby arrive home, if breastfeeding problems develop, skilled help is not always affordable or easy to find. When maternity leave ends, many women find their workplaces lack the support they need to continue breastfeeding.

> If you're in the U.S., see how the National Breastfeeding Center ranks your insurance company's breastfeeding benefits at: *http:// www.nbfcenter.com/PayerScorecard.html.*

At this writing, a recently upheld U.S. health care law, the Affordable Care Act, is now in place. According to this law, the costs of breastfeeding supplies and services for new mothers should be covered by health insurance. How this law's provisions will translate into reality is still unclear. As always, the devil is in the details.

Weaning earlier than intended, however, is not always the result of health care or worksite challenges. It has a much more personal side. Another major reason so many women stop nursing before they had planned is that they are confused about what's normal and how breastfeeding works

(DaMota, Banuelos, Goldbronn, Vera-Beccera, & Heinig, 2012). My hope is that this book will provide an antidote to this confusion so that you can experience the empowerment that comes from reaching your breastfeeding goals.

Maternity Leave

The length of your maternity leave is a big piece of this puzzle. Paid maternity leave is available in almost every country, but the details vary from place to place. In Sweden, for example, one year of paid maternity leave is standard, and fathers also have six months of paid leave. In Canada, depending on how long a mother has been at her job and how many hours per week she works, she may be eligible for 15 weeks of paid leave at full salary with an option to take up to 52 weeks at partial salary and her job guaranteed. Yet not all Canadian mothers take advantage of this.

In the U.K., mothers receive 90% of their weekly salary for the first six weeks after birth and the option of up to 52 weeks maternity leave. After the first six weeks, they can stay home at a flat rate for the next 33 weeks, and the last 13 weeks are unpaid. In Australia, 12 months unpaid leave is guaranteed, and the Australian government pays employers (who pass this on to mothers) up to 18 weeks of pay at the national minimum wage, in addition to whatever job benefits mothers receive. But even where paid maternity leave is available, some women do not take advantage of it.

In the United States, under the Family and Medical Leave Act, 12 weeks of unpaid leave is the law of the land, but that's only for those working full time in companies with more than 50 employees. For many American women, any maternity leave—paid or unpaid—is just a dream. But because maternity leave in the U.S. is tied to job benefits, some have more leeway than others. Women employed at the upper levels of large corporations may receive six months or more of paid leave, while women in low-income jobs may have no leave at all and be forced by money pressures to return to work within weeks—or even days—after giving birth.

How This Book Can Help

No matter where you live or what kind of work you do, knowing how the length of your maternity leave affects your back-to-work planning may give you a useful perspective. That's what the first chapter is about. Even if you have no say in your maternity leave, these insights will give you a better idea of what to expect. Hopefully, having this big picture will help you put the sometimes-confusing details into place.

This book can also help you better understand how breastfeeding works (Chapter 3), so that you can tell good advice from bad. It also explains how breastfeeding and bottle-feeding differ (Chapter 7). It describes how to choose a pump that fits you well and is suited to your situation (Chapter 4), how to make the most of your pumping time

(Chapter 5), what you need to know about storing and handling your milk (Chapter 6), specific tips for making bottle- and cup-feeding easier (Chapters 7 and 8), and ways to make the transition back to work easier (Chapter 9).

In addition to the practical details, this book addresses the sometimes-strong feelings you may have about returning to work (Chapter 10). Once you're back at work, it gives you the specifics you need for keeping your milk production stable over the long term (Chapter 11). As the months pass, it also covers how to troubleshoot your milk production as needed (Chapter 12), how your baby's growth affects working and breastfeeding, and when the time is right, how to make weaning both comfortable and positive (Chapter 13).

My fondest hope is that this book will help you achieve your personal breastfeeding goals. Especially during the early weeks, breastfeeding can sometimes feel like a marathon. But like a marathon, crossing the finish line can be a real peak experience. And like the effort that goes into preparing for a race, the more you put into your breastfeeding relationship, the more you can relish the elation that comes with such an outstanding achievement. Between now and then, I'll be cheering you on.

Nancy Mohrbacher
Arlington Heights, IL USA
December 2013

Back-to-Work Overview by Baby's Age

Throughout human history, women worked—and worked hard!—with their babies wrapped either against their bodies or safely nearby. In the 1800s, with the growth of cities and the rise of industry, women's work in the industrialized world changed radically. Instead of working alongside their children, many mothers left their little ones with others and went elsewhere to work. In factories and mills, children often worked too. For many, this cultural change transformed family life, and with it, breastfeeding.

Is it possible, in our modern world, to both be employed and fit breastfeeding into your life? The answer is most definitely yes. How do you do it? Technology continues to change the way men and women work, offering more options for working remotely. Some women find ways to work from home, which is covered in detail in the next chapter. When work involves leaving your baby, you might assume that you will need to use pumps and bottles. But as you will see in this chapter, that's not always so. Your baby's age is one of the major factors affecting breastfeeding when you return to work. Below, I've briefly outlined what you need to know about returning to work at various time windows during your baby's first year of life. If you're not sure how long to stay home after birth, this chapter may help you decide. If your maternity leave is already set, it describes what you can expect at different ages and stages. The main focus of this chapter is how the length of your maternity leave will likely affect breastfeeding and your daily routine.

Birth to 5 Weeks

Because you and your baby are most vulnerable during this stage, breastfeeding while starting work now is the most challenging. Even so, if you know the basics and plan ahead, you can meet your breastfeeding goals. If you have the option to stay home longer, seriously consider it.

Feeding Your Baby from Birth to 5 Weeks

Plan to feed your newborn only mother's milk or, as a substitute, infant formula. Most babies this age are fed by bottle. (In parts of developing countries, where the water is not safe, small straight-side cups or spoons are often used to feed babies this age because they can be cleaned more easily.) Most experts recommend delaying bottle feeds until at least 3 to 4 weeks of age to allow babies the time and practice to first get really good at breastfeeding (see Chapter 8 for more on this). But you can start earlier if you need to.

At this age, your newborn is unlikely to adjust well to any sort of feeding schedule. Experts agree that babies should be fed "on cue," meaning whenever they show feeding cues, signs that they are hungry, like rooting, hand-to-mouth, and fussing (AAP, 2012). The American Academy of Pediatrics describes crying as a late hunger cue, so it's best whenever possible to feed your baby before he begins to wail. In this fragile period (the start of what is sometimes called the "fourth trimester"), as your baby makes his transition to life outside the womb, he needs lots of holding and cuddling. Between 2 and 14 weeks, most babies are fussy for part of the day. Even when nothing seems to soothe your baby, it's important he be held and comforted. Hopefully, whoever is caring for your baby will be sensitive to his need for frequent feedings and carrying.

Figure 1-1. *Tiny babies need lots of feeding and holding.*

Expect your baby's feeding volumes, the amount he eats, to increase from birth to 5 weeks. His stomach is growing quickly, and his need for milk is increasing. During the first week, your newborn's stomach holds comfortably only about 1 oz. (30 mL) of milk, so if he gets bottles then, be sure not to overfeed (see Chapter 8 and the Caregiver handout, Appendix A, for specific tips on this). By the second week, breastfeeding babies consume on average about 1.5 oz. (45 mL) per feed. By the third week, feeding volume is up to 2 to 3 oz. (60 to 90 mL). By the fourth week, your baby will reach an average maximum feeding volume of 3 to 4 oz. (90 to 120 mL). This is about how much he will need to eat until it's time for him to start solids.

Breastfed babies typically take less milk more often than formula-fed babies (Sievers, Oldigs, Santer, & Schaub, 2002). Breastfed newborns average 8 to 12 feedings per day. Formula-fed newborns average 6 to 8 feedings per day. Whether your baby is breastfeeding or bottle-feeding, encourage small, frequent feeds, as large feedings put babies at higher risk of overweight and obesity later (Li, Fein, & Grummer-Strawn, 2008).

Your Comfort and Goals from Birth to 5 Weeks

When returning to work at or before 5 weeks, make it a top priority to take good care of yourself. At 5 weeks, you are still physically recovering from delivery, and that can take many weeks. In one study, of women at 5 weeks postpartum, breastfeeding mothers reported an average of six childbirth-related symptoms such as back pain, headaches, and fatigue (McGovern et al., 2006). Mothers who delivered by cesarean had more health problems at 5 weeks than those who delivered vaginally. It may also take a while for your energy to return to its normal level.

To stimulate a good milk supply during the early weeks, most babies breastfeed intensively, clustering their feedings close together during some parts of the day. Milk production reaches its peak at about 5 weeks. If you're not with your baby for these newborn feeding frenzies, what can you do to stimulate the milk production you need over the long term? Your decisions will, of course, depend on your goals.

If your goal is to provide your milk exclusively for your baby, you first and foremost need to know how milk production works. The key dynamic is how many times each day the milk is removed well from your breasts, either by breastfeeding or pumping. More milk removals stimulate more milk production. Fewer milk removals tells your body to produce less milk. The time interval between milk removals is not important, with one exception: avoid going so long between milk removals that your breasts feel full, because getting full causes milk production to slow. (Drained breasts make milk faster, and full breasts make milk slower.) Focus on your 24-hour milk-removal total and know that it is fine now to breastfeed or pump very, very often to boost supply. A good goal is 10 or more milk removals per day. I will explain this process in more detail in Chapter 3.

During the first two weeks after birth, babies breast-feed, on average, nine times every 24 hours, and during the four weeks that follow, they average eight feedings every 24 hours (Hill, Aldag, Chatterton, & Zinaman, 2005). When you're not with your baby, you can pump often to try to reach your daily milk-removal goals. Breastfeeding or pumping even more often will get you to your goal even faster. On average, by about 5 weeks, babies consume between 25 and 30 oz. (750 to 900 mL) of milk per day, which is the most they'll ever need. If you can get your milk production up to 30 oz. (900 mL) per day, you'll be making enough milk for your baby's entire first year. Then all you need to do is keep it steady, which requires a lot less work.

Full-Time Work

When you start working full time between birth and 5 weeks, plan to fit in your 10 milk removals per day however it works best for you. Depending on the situation, some might find it easier to breastfeed nine times while at home and pump once during their work day. Others might find more pumping at work easier. Keep in mind that there's nothing magical about the time intervals between milk removals. They don't have to be evenly spaced. Pumping or breastfeeding every hour workstoo. At this stage, a gap of up to six hours once per day is fine. What matters most to your milk production is the total number of daily milk removals and how fully the milk is removed. Breanna describes how she was able to maintain her milk production after returning to work at three weeks postpartum.

> I am a breastfeeding mom who works full time in the legal department of a collection agency. I started work when my daughter was just 3 weeks old. I began using a breast pump at home, prior to returning to work, to stock up on milk. Physically it was hard to return to work because my breasts ached, never feeling like pumping got me "empty" enough. With breastfeeding I never felt that way. After returning to work, I arranged with my boss two 10-minute pumping breaks and one 30-minute break, but I began to notice my milk supply dropping. I decided to start pumping while at home too. I breastfeed throughout the nights and on weekends, which have taken on a whole new meaning to me. I look forward to continuing them for as long as possible.
> —*Breanna W., Washington State, USA*

If exclusive breastfeeding is not your goal, you can leave infant formula as a substitute for as many feedings as needed, and breastfeed when you and your baby are together. Some breastfeeding is always better than none.

Part-Time Work

From birth to 5 weeks, just like at other stages, working fewer hours per week gives you more flexibility. Your need to pump at work will depend on your work schedule.

If you're away from your baby for no longer than about six hours (including travel time), it may work well to simply breastfeed before you leave, after you get home, and fit in your 10 milk removals while you're with your baby. Rather than expressing milk at work, if your goal is to leave only your milk for your baby, you might instead pump at home right after or 30 to 60 minutes after some feedings to store extra milk for work days. (I describe guidelines for milk storage and handling in Chapter 6.)

If your part-time work schedule involves working fewer long days, you may need to express your milk at work in order to stay comfortable and meet your long-term goals. (See Appendix C for sample plans for different work schedules.)

6 Weeks to 3 Months

Many mothers in the U.S. return to work when their babies are between 6 weeks and 3 months. This can also be true for women who live in countries that offer longer paid maternity leave. Depending on circumstances, some mothers outside the U.S. begin work now.

Feeding Your Baby from 6 Weeks to 3 Months

Plan to feed your baby younger than 6 months mother's milk or, as a substitute, infant formula. When a baby this age is not breastfed, he will most likely be bottle-fed. Expect your baby's feeding pattern to change during the part of the day that he gets his feedings by bottle. In Chapter 7, I provide more details on how breast and bottle differ, and Chapter 8, I suggest ways to make bottle-feeding more like breastfeeding.

Your Comfort and Goals from 6 Weeks to 3 Months

Make it a top priority to take good care of yourself. At this stage, many women have not yet fully recovered from childbirth. One study found that at 11 weeks, women reported an average of four childbirth-related symptoms, such as pain and fatigue (McGovern et al., 2007). Another study found that women in the U.S. who had less than 12 weeks of maternity leave were at greater risk for symptoms of depression (Chatterji & Markowitz, 2012). This is the time to ask for help. Don't try to be superwoman.

When it comes to your milk supply, there is good news. As mentioned, if your baby has been exclusively breastfed and is gaining weight well, you should now be at full milk production. Breastfed babies' milk intake stays remarkably stable between 5 weeks and 6 months, varying only by about 2 to 4 oz. (60 to 120 mL) per day (Nielsen et al., 2011). What this means is that you don't have to worry about your baby needing more milk later as he grows. All you have to do is maintain the milk production you have now. (See more on this in Chapter 11.) If you want your baby to receive only your milk for the first six months, this means you just need to focus on keeping your milk production stable.

At 6 months, your baby's need for milk will begin to decrease when he starts eating solid foods.

Full-Time Work

If your goal is to provide your milk only for your 6-week-to-3-month-old baby, before returning to work full-time (32 or more hours per week), count how many times each 24-hour period your baby breastfed while you were on maternity leave. This number, which varies among mothers, gives you an idea of how many times you should remove milk each day from your breasts (your "milk removals"), via breastfeeding and/or pumping, to keep your milk production stable over the long term. These milk removals do not have to be at regular time intervals, such as every two hours. The time between milk removals can vary during the day. I will describe this more in Chapter 11. Joy describes how many times she needs to pump at work to maintain her milk production.

> I went back to work full-time as an assistant project manager for a construction company when my son was 2 months old. I pump three times at work as well as right before I leave for work; and now at 11 months I still nurse at night and weekends.
> —*Joy S, Kentucky, USA*

Since you need to remove milk from your breasts a certain number of times each day, you might think about how you can make that easier. For example, is it possible to find a caregiver close to work rather than close to home so that you can breastfeed during your work day? If not, plan how many times each day you'll need to pump. With this number as a starting point, you can then customize your routine. I give more details on how to make this all work in chapters that follow.

If you do not plan to provide your milk for all missed feedings, you can leave infant formula as a substitute for as many feedings as needed, and breastfeed when you and your baby are together. As I described earlier, some breastfeeding is better than none. Breastfeeding doesn't have to be all or nothing.

Part-Time Work

As babies grow and mature, they become more adaptable. Work options that give you more flexibility during the 6-weeks-to-3-month stage (and the previous stage, too) will make it much easier for both you and your baby to adjust.

Your work schedule and your goals will determine whether you need to express milk at work. If your work day is six hours or less, even if you plan to give your milk exclusively, you may not need to pump at work. If you work longer days, you may have to. In Appendix C, I provide some sample plans for different work schedules.

4 to 5 Months

Your baby is now beginning to be more aware of his sur-roundings—and of you. When your baby smiles and plays while he nurses, this can be lots of fun.

Feeding Your Baby from 4 to 5 Months

In years past, many mothers were told to introduce sol-ids when their babies were 4 or 5 months old. You might have started solid foods at this age. However, major health organizations, such as the World Health Organization, have changed their recommendations and are now telling moth-ers to wait a little longer, and not introduce solids until their babies are at least 6 months old. When your baby is in this age range, just keep doing what you've been doing.

What to Feed

From birth to 6 months, health experts now recommend babies be fed only mother's milk or, as a substitute, infant formula (AAP, 2012; WHO, 2010). Researchers have found that there are health drawbacks to both mother and baby when solids are introduced before the age of 6 months (Kramer & Kakuma, 2012). For example, babies who start solids at this age are at greater risk for digestive problems, and mothers lose less weight.

At this age, an average 24-hour milk intake for an exclusively breastfeeding baby is about 25 to 30 oz. (750 to 900 mL). As at other ages, daily milk intake is much greater among formula-fed babies, so don't gauge your breastfed baby's need for milk by what a formula-fed baby consumes. Breast and bottle differ. I describe these differences in more detail in Chapter 7.

How to Feed

When a 4-to 5-month-old baby can't be breastfed, he will most likely be bottle-fed, although some babies this age can master sippy cups. It's common for babies to take more milk from the bottle, and feed fewer times per day, than when they're home and breastfeeding. While at home, expect your baby to breastfeed as often as when he was younger (Kent et al., 2006). Unlike formula-fed babies, many breastfed babies' feeding patterns don't change much between 1 and 6 months.

Your Comfort & Goals from 4 to 5 Months

Women who start back to work after 12 weeks are more likely to breastfeed longer than those who return to work sooner (Ogbuanu, Glover, Probst, Liu, & Hussey, 2011). Why? At 3 months, your milk production is well established, and maintaining supply is easier than increasing it. Your household stress levels may be lower, because your baby has outgrown the evening fussy periods that are so common in younger babies. Women whose maternity leave is three months or longer may also have more flexible and supportive working conditions, making continued breast-feeding easier (Skafida, 2012).

If you've been exclusively breastfeeding up to now, you have been at full milk production since about 5 weeks (Hill et al., 2005). If you want your baby to receive your milk only, all you have to do moving forward is maintain your supply until your baby starts solids and his need for milk decreas-es. To make this happen, it's important to know how your actions affect your milk production. (I describe this more in Chapter 11.) As mentioned before, the key dynamic is your number of daily milk removals (breastfeeds plus pumps). Knowing how milk production works also allows you to adjust your milk supply up or down as needed. Being clear on the differences between breast and bottle (see Chapter 7) can also help you distinguish good advice from bad.

Full-Time Work

At 4 to 5 months, if you'll be working 32 or more hours a week, you can decide how many times each work day to pump by counting the number of hours you'll be away from your baby (include your travel time). Try not to go longer than about three hours between milk removals. You can then customize your routine with the suggestions in Chapter 11. If there's a way you can breastfeed during your longest break at work (going to your baby or having your baby brought to you), that can greatly simplify your life. For Kimberly, seeing her baby during the work day also helped ease her emotional transition back to work.

> I returned to work full-time as a teacher when my son was 4.5 months old. I was fortunate that our caregiver lived close to our school. I went to see my baby on my break. I nursed him and took him on walks, held him until he fell asleep. Those times saved my sanity, soothed my broken heart, helped me feel connected to him despite leaving him each day. And at night and on the weekends, I savored my time with him, squeezing in all my love and memory-making into those off-the-clock hours which never seemed long enough.
>
> —*Kimberly P., Texas, USA*

At this stage, like the others, if you do not plan to provide your milk for all missed feedings, you can leave infant formula as a substitute for as many feedings as needed and breastfeed when you and your baby are together. Some breastfeeding is always better than none.

Part-Time Work

In Appendix C, I describe sample plans for different work schedules. At every stage, working part time gives you more flexibility, which makes breastfeeding easier.

6 to 8 Months

At this age, babies are learning to sit up and feed themselves. It's so exciting to watch your baby grow and learn new skills!

Feeding Your Baby from 6 to 8 Months

Experts now recommend starting solid foods at 6 months (AAP, 2012; WHO, 2010). This is a good time to introduce your baby to the foods you serve at your family table.

What to Feed

There is no one right way to start solid foods. Families worldwide offer their babies different foods at different times. To make your choices, consider what is grown locally and what foods are in season. The fresher and less processed your baby's foods, the tastier and more nutritious they will be.

Although your baby may start solid foods at about 6 months, most babies this age are just learning this new way of eating and are not yet consuming very much. This means your milk (or infant formula as a substitute) will still be your baby's main food. At this age, in 24 hours an average breastfeeding baby consumes about 25 to 30 oz. (750 to 900 mL) of milk. Formula-fed babies this age consume about 25% more milk each day (Heinig, Nommsen, Peerson, Lonnerdal, & Dewey, 1993).

How to Feed

This is a good age to start solids because babies are learning to sit up and can take an active role in feeding themselves. To learn more about how to make this easier, see the book, *Baby-Led Weaning: The Essential Guide to Introducing Solid Foods - and Helping Your Baby to Grow Up a Happy and Confident Eater*, by Gill Rapley and Tracey Murkett or its mobile phone app.

Figure 1-2. *As babies grow, they can take an active role in feeding themselves.*

Most 6-to-8-month-old babies are not yet drinking well from a cup, so if your baby misses a breastfeed, he will most likely be bottle-fed. An average breastfeeding baby this age takes about 3 to 4 oz. (90 to 120 mL) at the breast. Babies fed by bottle tend to drink more milk per feeding and feed fewer times per day. If your baby bottle-feeds while you're at work, don't be surprised if his feeding pattern changes during that part of the day. If your baby takes more milk from the bottle than you can pump, this may simply be due to the differences in the milk delivery system. I will talk more about how feeding patterns differ by breast and bottle, and how to prevent overfeeding with the bottle in Chapters 7 and 8.

Your Comfort and Goals from 6 to 8 Months

When your baby is 6 to 8 months old, your milk production may start to decrease slightly as your baby begins taking solid foods (Islam, Peerson, Ahmed, Dewey, & Brown, 2006). But you will not likely notice a difference in breastfeeding patterns when you and your baby are together. Your comfort during your work day, and your long-term milk production, will depend on regular milk removals by either breastfeeding or pumping.

If you are starting back to work now, your work situation and your breastfeeding goals will affect your choices. Whatever else you decide to do, you can breastfeed when you and your baby are together.

Full-Time Work

At 6 to 8 months, if your baby's been exclusively breastfed (except for some solids), and you want your baby to have your milk for all missed feedings, start by trying not to go more than three hours at work without pumping. (See Chapter 11 for ways to customize your work day pumping routine and for an overview of what determines your milk production long term.)

If you will not be providing your milk for all missed feedings, you can leave infant formula as a substitute for as many feedings as needed and breastfeed when you and your baby are together. Again, breastfeeding doesn't have to be all or nothing.

Part-Time Work

Working fewer hours per week gives you more flexibility. Your need to pump at work will depend on your schedule. If you work short days and you're away from your baby for no longer than about six hours, you may not need to pump at work. To provide your milk for work days, you can pump at convenient times at home.

If you're working fewer long days, you may need to express your milk at work to stay comfortable. (See Appendix C for sample plans for different work schedules.)

9 to 11 Months

This is a time of rapid growth and development, with your baby crawling, pulling up, and maybe even learning to walk. Many mothers who started work when their babies were younger begin phasing out pumping now (Ortiz, McGilligan, & Kelly, 2004).

Feeding Your Baby from 9 to 11 Months

Your baby still needs milk during your work day, but because he is also eating solid food, he needs less milk now than he did when he was younger.

What to Feed

Until your baby reaches one year, health experts recommend you continue to provide mother's milk or, as a substitute, infant formula (AAP, 2012; WHO, 2010). If you started your baby on solid foods at 6 months, your baby is probably gradually taking more and more solids and, as a result, consuming less and less milk (Islam et al., 2006).

How to Feed

By about 9 months of age, your baby can start drinking from a cup, making bottles optional. Try a few of the different styles of baby cups to find those that your baby likes best (for details, see Chapter 8). Most babies this age can sit up and easily feed themselves finger foods and larger pieces with natural "handles," such as cooked broccoli stalks.

It is common for babies this age to become much faster and more efficient at breastfeeding than when they were younger. Don't be surprised if your baby takes a lot of milk in just a few minutes. As long as your baby is growing and gaining weight well, short feedings are not a cause for concern.

Your Comfort and Goals from 9 to 11 Months

During your baby's second 6 months, expect your milk production to begin to slowly decrease as your baby takes more solids. If your baby drinks only your milk while you're at work, you may notice over time that you are pumping less milk per session. This is a normal part of your baby's transition from a milk-only diet to one that includes solid foods. (See Chapter 13 for more on this.) However, to stay comfortable at work and to keep your milk production where you want it, you'll need to keep an eye on your total number of milk removals (breastfeeds plus pumps) each day. The number of milk removals per day needed to keep milk production stable varies by mother. (For more on this, see the Chapter 11 section on the Magic Number.)

No matter what your work situation is, you can breastfeed when you and your baby are together. Your other options depend on how many hours per week you work and your goals.

Full-Time Work

If you start working full-time (32 or more hours per week) when your baby is 9 to 11 months old, your pumping and feeding choices will depend on your milk production and your goals. If your baby has been exclusively breastfed (except for solid foods), and you want your baby to have your milk for all missed feedings, you may begin by going no longer than about three hours between pumping or breastfeeding at work. (See Chapter 11 for how to customize your pumping routine during your work day.)

At this and the previous stages, there are ways to structure your day to minimize the amount of milk you need to leave for your baby. If you need less milk, this also means less pumping, which is always a plus. (See the section "Impact of Daily Routines" in Chapter 11 for details). If your baby is near your workplace, you can also breastfeed during the day rather than pump, as Michelle found.

> I returned to work full-time as a newspaper reporter when my second daughter was 10 months old. My husband had decided to stay home and care for our children while I worked. As we lived close to my place of work at the time, this was ideal for us. I could return home for lunch to breastfeed. If I breastfed her before I left for work, at lunchtime and when I came home, she was not missing out on any feedings at all.
>
> —*Michelle P., Newfoundland, Canada*

If you do not plan to provide your milk for all missed feedings, you can leave infant formula as a substitute for as many feedings as needed, and breastfeed when you and your baby are together. Breastfeeding does not have to be all or nothing. Some breastfeeding is always better than none for both you and your baby.

If you've been back to work for a while and want to phase out pumping now, to reduce the risk of pain and breast problems, see Chapter 13 for how to make these changes gradually and comfortably.

Part-Time Work

Working part time rather than full-time when your baby is 9 to 11 months old gives you more flexibility, which makes breastfeeding easier. Your need to pump at work will depend on your work schedule. If you're away from your baby for no longer than six hours or so, one option is to simply breastfeed before you leave and after you get home. Rather than having to express milk at work, if you want to leave only your milk for your baby, you might instead pump at convenient times while home to store milk for work days. (See Chapter 9 for when to pump at home without impacting your baby's need for milk.)

If you're working fewer long days, however, you may need to pump at work to stay comfortable. (See Appendix C for sample plans for different work schedules.)

12 Months or Older

From a breastfeeding standpoint, there are many advantages to returning to work after your baby turns 1 year.

Feeding Your Baby after 12 Months

At this stage, pumping and bottles are not required. You can simply breastfeed when you and your baby are together, and leave other foods and drinks for baby when you are apart.

What to Feed

While you're at work, your baby can eat as much solid foods as he likes and whatever drinks you choose. Chances are your baby has been eating solid foods for at least six months. The only solids to avoid are those that could be a choking hazard, such as uncut grapes, hot dogs, and raw carrots. Your baby is old enough to drink cow's milk straight from the dairy case, as well as water and other milks. Unlike when your baby was younger, at this age you don't have to provide your milk (or infant formula as a substitute) while you're away. Some mothers decide they prefer to leave their milk at this stage. It's just one of many choices.

How to Feed

At one year, your baby should be drinking well from whichever type of baby cup he prefers. This means bottles are optional. If you like, your baby can go directly from breast to cup without using bottles at all. The advantage of this approach is that there's no need to wean again from bottles later. Most babies this age have had ample practice feeding themselves solid foods and need little help at mealtimes and snacks.

Your Comfort and Goals after 12 Months

Solid foods and drinks take the place of your milk in baby's diet, so during your baby's second 6 months, expect your milk production to slow gradually as your baby eats more solids. (See Chapter 13 for more on how this works.) By one year, your milk production may have decreased enough so that even without pumping, you feel no breast fullness during your work day. If you do feel full when you first start work, as needed you can express just enough milk to make yourself comfortable. As long as you don't fully drain your breasts at work, you will probably only need to "pump to comfort" for a short time as your milk production adjusts, as Crystal describes.

> I went back to work when the youngest of my three daughters was 12 months old. At that point, she was still breastfeeding on demand, and demanding she was! :) She loved to breastfeed! It took my breasts a good week to not get so full during the day. Every day at 2 o'clock I would think only three more hours until I can feed her.
>
> —*Crystal N., Manitoba, Canada*

You've reached the happy stage where breastfeeding and milk production require little thought or planning on your part. Whether you're working full-time or part-time, you won't need to pump during your work day unless you're away from your baby for an unusually long time, such as overnight work travel. At some point, because all children eventually outgrow breastfeeding, your baby will wean from the breast. The timing is up to you and your baby. The longer you breastfeed, the healthier for both of you. If you are thinking about weaning, see Chapter 13 for weaning strategies that are gentle and comfortable.

Now that you have a sense of how returning to work at different stages affects breastfeeding, in Chapter 2, let's take a close look at work and childcare options. It may help you to know how these variables may affect your plans, and how the type of work you do and your work setting may make a difference.

Job Specifics, Family Differences, and Childcare

Knowing how the length of your maternity leave affects back-to-work breastfeeding planning gives you a good first glimpse of the big picture. Next, let's focus on how job specifics, family differences, and childcare may affect breastfeeding. This chapter covers full-time, part-time, and flexible job options, work travel, as well as working from home. It also covers how to talk to your boss about breastfeeding (yikes!) and dealing with challenging work settings. It explores some of the unique aspects of breastfeeding when you're single, low income, or have a same-sex partner. In addition, it covers how childcare choices may affect breastfeeding, and provides questions to ask when shopping for a childcare provider.

Job Status, Options, and Settings

Your work setting and job status may influence your options. As an example of job status, some jobs pay by the hour and provide no paid time off or other benefits. In some parts of the world, they are called "casual" or "hourly" jobs, or you may work as an "independent contractor." If you don't show up to work, you may lose your job. Some jobs are very structured, even requiring you punch a time clock. Others are salaried, which may involve much unpaid overtime. Some positions have lots of room to maneuver, and some have rigid expectations. But even if your job is not flexible, it's good to be aware of some of the possibilities, especially if the job you have now makes breastfeeding challenging.

Part-Time or Full-Time Work

The number of hours you work each week, whether full- or part-time, can affect breastfeeding. For our purposes, let's define part-time as less than 32 hours per week. Full-time is typically more than 32 hours per week.

Part-Time Work

Working part time makes it easier for many mothers to breastfeed longer and more exclusively. On average, breastfeeding mothers who work part-time nurse as long as mothers who are not employed (Ogbuanu, Glover, Probst, Hussey, & Liu, 2011). Not surprisingly, as daily work hours increase, mothers are less likely to exclusively breastfeed (Roe, Whittington, Fein, & Teisl, 1999).

Part-time work includes a variety of work schedules that affect breastfeeding differently. For example, if you work fewer long days (eight hours or more), it may be easier to keep your milk production steady if you alternate work days with days at home. If there's any dip in milk production, your baby can bring it up to speed with intensive nursing while you're together. If you work four days per week, it may help to schedule your home day in the middle. An advantage of long days is that you may have more days at home.

But working short days has advantages, too. For example, if your baby is younger than 1 year and your work day (including travel time) is no longer than the longest stretch between feedings while you were on maternity leave (maybe four to six hours), you may not need to pump at work to maintain milk production. If you have a young baby, any milk your baby needs during your work day you can pump at home after feedings.

Some mothers alternate between working part-time and full-time. Some work full-time during their company's busy season and part-time at other times of the year. If this sounds like you, see Chapter 11 and Appendix C for suggestions for maintaining milk production with different schedules.

Full-Time Work

Breastfeeding and working full time (32 or more hours per week) is more of a challenge, but many women have proved it can be done. Studies around the world have found that among mothers returning to work full-time when their babies are younger than 6 months, fewer breastfeed at all, and on average those who do breastfeed nurse for a shorter time.

If you'll be working full-time, don't despair. This simply means you need to be better prepared than mothers who work part time. You need to understand how milk production works and the effects of your daily choices on how much milk you make. These specifics are in the chapters to come.

Flexible Work Arrangements

Along with part-time and full-time options, let's add flexible work arrangements to the mix. It just might be possible for you to incorporate one of these options into your work life. Even if you think your job has little flexibility, you may have more than you realize. Here are some arrangements to consider.

- **Job-sharing**—Sharing one position with another person (another mother?)

- **Phase back**—Gradually increasing work hours from part time to full time

- **Compressed work week**—Working the same hours in fewer days

- **Telecommuting**—Working from home, either some or all of your work days

- **On-site daycare**—Going to baby for feedings

- **Bring baby to work**—Keep your baby with you while you are working. For resources, see the excellent *www.parentingatwork.org* and *www.babiesatwork. org*

- **Flex-time**—Adjusting work hours to your baby's routine

As an example of flex time, my friend René decided to go back to work part time as a waitress to help make ends meet after her third child was born. She asked her supervisor for the late shift, so her work hours coincided with her baby's longest sleep stretch. She didn't have to pump, and her baby didn't need to be fed while she was at work. That scheduling inspiration simplified working and breastfeeding for her.

Working from Home

The work-from-home option deserves special attention because lots of mothers do it. It has advantages and its own unique challenges.

Many of us enter motherhood with unrealistic ideas of how long babies actually sleep during the day, and how many other tasks we can accomplish. It is often a huge surprise to discover how much time baby care really takes. How do mothers employed from home manage? These are some examples of work-from-home mothers who I knew personally, or who have written about their experiences.

Figure 2-1. *Working from home, even part time, can make breastfeeding easier.*

- Melissa, a public relations coordinator, hired a caregiver to care for her baby in her home while she worked full-time. Her baby was brought to her for some, but not all, feedings. Melissa provided pumped milk for the other feedings.

- Carmen, a telemarketer, worked full-time from home and hired a caregiver who lived across the street. The caregiver brought the baby to Carmen for all feedings.

- Kirsten, a scientist, worked part time at home two days a week with a neighborhood teen tending to her baby during her eight-hour shifts, bringing the baby to her for all feedings.

- Rosa, an IT specialist, worked part time at home two days a week and at the office two days a week. At home, she completed her work tasks during her baby's nap times and in the evening when her partner spent time with the baby.

- Swati, a business-owner, began working from home when her baby was two weeks old, using her laptop as her baby slept or nursed. She took the baby to her office once a week until her baby was a little older, when a friend tended to her baby three hours per day, three days per week while she went to the office.

My own work-from-home experience involved learning how to type I while I breastfed my youngest son, Ben, as I wrote my first breastfeeding counseling guide for professionals.

Jennifer Bowen Hicks, in her book, *Hirkani's Daughters,* describes tips for making working from home more pleasant for everyone (Hicks, 2006).

- Make it fun (rotate toys available during work hours, use a baby carrier, keep your mood positive by making sure to eat regularly and well, and scheduling some down time).

- Make it fair (try to pick work hours when your child is happiest or asleep, give your child attention during work breaks, limit the of use swings and play yards, and make sure your baby is well fed).

- Tap into your community (enlist the help of supporters such as other working parents, teen aides, and relatives).

Work Travel

I've known many mothers who have traveled extensively for work, yet have still managed to meet their breastfeeding goals. Some of them brought their baby and a caregiver with them on trips, which obviously made breastfeeding easier. Jessica is a full-time consultant who works with colleges and universities on their software systems. Most of those in similar positions travel every week Sunday through Thursday, but not Jessica.

> I'm blessed to work for a company that embraces web meetings and arranges for its consultants to travel just once a month to the client. My work is contract based and quite often anywhere from three to 12 months at a time with just one client to support. I am fortunate that on my salary we can afford to have my husband be the stay-at-home parent. I began working from home when my son was 6 weeks old. I still had office hours to keep but was able to have baby on my lap to nurse & sleep. When my

baby was 5 months, I started to the client for a week of work each month, my husband and son traveled with me so that I could nurse instead of pump.

—*Jessica E., Illinois, USA*

But many women do not have this option. How can you make breastfeeding work if you're away from your baby for days at a time? These are the basic ingredients.

- **Understand how milk production works.** Thankfully this isn't hard. See Chapter 3.

- **Know your "magic number."** You need more than generalities. You need to know how many milk removals (breastfeeds plus pumps) per day you need in order to keep your milk production steady. To determine this, see Chapters 9 and 11.

- **Be able to effectively express your milk.** See Chapter 5.

Pre-planning can also help. For example, before arriving at your travel destination, if possible, arrange for pumping breaks during your work day. Most mothers don't have to pump during their sleep hours at night. You may be able to pump last thing before bed and first thing when you awaken.

If you'll be flying, should you check your pump at the airport? If you do, you run the risk of losing it. If you carry it on the airplane, you don't have much room for anything else. An alternative is to check your double electric pump and include a manual pump in your carry-on bag, just in case. If you're traveling for work without your baby, and you are trying to decide what to do with your pumped milk while you're away, see the "Options While Traveling Without Baby" section of Chapter 6.

> U.S. mothers can read FAQ about the protection the law provides them for pumping at work at: *http://www.dol.gov/whd/nursingmothers/faqBT-NM.htm*

Challenging Work Settings

There's no doubt that breastfeeding and pumping are easier in some job settings than others. Office workers, especially those with private offices, usually find it simpler to fit pumping into their work day than letter carriers, waitresses, hair stylists, farm and construction workers, and mothers serving in the military. (If you're in the U.S. military, be sure to check into your new rights under the Affordable Care Act, and see Robyn Roche-Paull's wonderful book, *Breastfeeding in Combat Boots*.) One study found that mothers in administrative and manual jobs stopped breastfeeding earlier than average, while women in service and professional jobs breastfed as long as non-employed mothers (Kimbro, 2006). Even in challenging work settings, many women find ways to have long and satisfying breastfeeding relationships, and you can, too!

Every job is different. Is your issue privacy? No break times? What most mothers need is actually very simple: a clean, private place to pump and two or three breaks of 20 minutes or more. (In the U.S., recent changes to the Fair Labor and Standards Act provide mothers with legal protections for pumping breaks. For details, see the later section "Preparing for That Talk.") If you have one of the following jobs, or one with similar challenges, these tips may help.

Teacher. To pump with little privacy and few breaks may require some creativity. Can you pump before your classes start in the morning? How about before you leave home in the morning? Is there a storeroom or an empty office in your building where you can pump during your lunch break? If your travel time is long, how about pumping after your students leave for the day?

Letter carrier/delivery person. Where to pump? Is there a clean, private space in the back of your truck where you can use a battery-operated breast pump? Many quality double pumps have a battery option. Do you deliver to a business with a lactation room you can use?

Salesperson/ home health care provider. If your job involves traveling to customers or patients, this can make finding a private place to pump tough. Is it possible to make a stop to breastfeed your baby a part of your work day? Although not ideal (especially in cold weather!), some women make their car their pumping home base. Privacy can be achieved by putting up a folding window shade in the front window, and closing a towel or baby blanket in the side windows to block the view. Some pumps take rechargeable batteries and have optional vehicle power adapters.

What are your options when for whatever reason you have a full-time job or work long days at a part-time job and will not be pumping? Amazingly, you still have many. For details, see the section "If You Won't Be Pumping at Work" in Chapter 9. The most important thing to keep in mind is that breastfeeding doesn't have to be all or nothing and that some breastfeeding is always better than none. Some mothers breastfeed when they're with their baby and give expressed milk or formula when they're not. Some use their maternity leave to pump like crazy so they have a large reserve of milk before returning to work and give this stored milk for as long as possible. After returning to work, others pump after feedings when they get home and on their days off, so they can provide at least some mother's milk feedings during their work week. Others give formula while they're away and breastfeed when they're together. If you choose this last option, see the "Partial Weaning" section in Chapter 9 on how to do this safely and comfortably.

Talking to Your Employer

Does the idea of talking to your boss about breastfeeding worry you? Many women are understandably intimidated by the thought of a work-related conversation involving their breasts, even if their boss is a woman. Some worry that asking for a time and place to breastfeed or pump will be seen as requesting special favors, even though companies benefit as much as families. In the U.S., it's now the law that mothers must be given the time and a place to pump that is not a bathroom. (See the next section for details.) The following tips may help you feel more comfortable about having this conversation.

Figure 2-2. *A job in a male-dominated industry may make talking to your boss about breastfeeding feel even more challenging.*

Assuming you're returning to the same job you had during pregnancy, it's best to discuss your post-baby breast-feeding-related needs with your supervisor before you go on maternity leave. If you live in the U.K., in order to receive your maternity benefits, the government requires that at least 15 weeks before your baby is due you tell your employer that you are pregnant and when you want your paid maternity leave to begin. In the U.S., this is the perfect time to discuss how best to combine all of your owed time off (personal days, vacation days, state pregnancy disability allowances, other short-term disability options, etc.) to lengthen your maternity leave. Before scheduling this talk, a little preparation may help.

Preparing for That Talk

Before you sit down to discuss your post-baby needs, first ask your co-workers if any other women have breast-fed while working there. If so, ask about their experiences. If your company has a human resources department, ask its staff if a lactation program exists, and if so, what it includes. If you're the first in your workplace to ask, you'll be a trailblazer, which may require more work and diplomacy. But if many of these issues have already been addressed, it may be a simple of matter of taking advantage of an existing program.

Second, check your national, state, or provincial laws. In the U.S., the Affordable Care Act (ACA) included a 2010 amendment to the Fair Labor Standards Act (FLSA) that provided new protections to employed breastfeeding moth-ers. What does this Reasonable Break Time for Nursing Mothers law require of employers?

- They must provide employees with babies less than 1 year old reasonable time to pump (two to three pumping breaks during an 8-hour work shift), which may be unpaid unless other employees receive paid breaks (Martin, 2011).

- Breastfeeding employees must have access to a place to pump other than a bathroom that is shielded from view and free from interruption by others.

This law does not cover breastfeeding. It only covers pumping. It does not require employers to provide pumps or refrigeration for pumped milk, but they must give mothers enough space to store pumping equipment and a milk cooler.

Also, this law applies only to those in FLSA non-exempt jobs. (FLSA status is listed on U.S. pay stubs.) Most jobs that pay by the hour are non-exempt and subject to this law. If you have a salaried position (do not receive overtime pay), this law likely does not cover you. It applies to employers with fewer than 50 employees, as well as larger employers. Companies with fewer than 50 employees have the option of applying for an "undue hardship" exemption if the law's requirements may negatively affect business. What's key for you to know here is that the burden of proof for undue hardship is on the company, not you. This federal law does not preempt state laws and some states provide even more protection. Check U.S. state laws at *http://www.ncsl.org/issues-research/health/breastfeeding-state-laws.aspx# State*

It's important to be aware of the law. But when talking to your boss, you also want to be careful not to talk about it in a way that is perceived as a veiled threat. Keep your main focus on the positive, as your company will benefit by supporting lactation.

The Making It Work for Moms brochure in the Making It Work Toolkit at: *http://www.dol.gov/whd/nursingmothers/faqBTNM.htm* includes a "My Lactation and Work Plan" page that is ideal for sharing with employers. It also includes a "How to Talk with Your Supervisor" section with specific suggestions for how to bring up your post-baby needs. This toolkit also includes a brochure for employers.

I will plan to use my usual breaks and lunch period to express milk. It will take around 20 minutes each time. If I need a little more time while I'm first learning, would you be open to letting me come in a little earlier to staying just a little later to make up the time?

—*Making It Work for Moms, New York State Department of Health*

Many employers know that the law requires them to support breastfeeding in the workplace. But if a U.S. employer is unwilling to provide these basic workplace protections, you can file a complaint at: *http://www.dol.gov/wecanhelp/howtofilecomplaint.htm*.

Lactation Support Is a Win-Win

About 30% of large U.S. companies offer some type of lactation support (SHRM, 2013). Companies invest in breastfeeding because studies have found that every $1 businesses spend on lactation saves them $3 (Cohen & Mrtek, 1994). The U.S. government's free toolkit, *The Business Case for Breastfeeding* (download it at: *http://www.womenshealth.gov/breastfeeding/government-in-action/business-case-for-breastfeeding*) describes three ways worksite lactation support saves businesses money (HRSA, 2008):

1. Breastfeeding employees miss less work. One-day work absences occur three times more often among mothers of formula-fed babies (Cohen, Mrtek, & Mrtek, 1995).

2. Breastfeeding lowers health care costs. In one company, health care costs were $2,146 per year higher among employees who did not participate in its lactation program (Ortiz, McGilligan, & Kelly, 2004).

3. With worksite lactation support, there is less employee turnover.

This last cost saving can be huge. When an employee decides to leave her position, it costs on average about 20% of her salary to replace her (Boushey & Glynn, 2012). In the U.S., employee retention after birth is 59%. In companies with lactation programs, the retention rate is as high as 94% (Ortiz et al., 2004).

If you discover you are the first in your workplace to ask about worksite lactation support, it might be helpful to know the most common employer barriers to providing it and some helpful responses.

- **Time away from work duties**. Let your boss know that you can pump during regular breaks and meal-times. If needed, you can come in early or leave late. Also, the need to pump at work is temporary, usually ending by baby's first birthday (Slusser, Lange, Dickson, Hawkes, & Cohen, 2004).

- **Discomfort with breastfeeding.** Choose your words carefully. Say "lactation" rather than "breastfeed-ing," and avoid sharing materials with nursing photos. People who've had no exposure to breastfeeding may be easily put off. If you know other women in your workplace who have worked and breastfed, get their permission to share their stories to show the larger need.

- **Resistance from other employees.** Include others in planning, and provide staff training, so everyone understands how the company benefits. Some companies also provide lactation support to partners of male employees in the form of discounted or free pumps, breastfeeding classes, phone help, even lactation home visits (Cohen, Lange, & Slusser, 2002).

- **Lack of available space.** If you don't have a private office, a pumping space can be as small as 4 by 5 feet

(1.5 by 2 meters), such as a modified storage room. Another option is a portable screen in a break room, office, or locker room to create a private area.

When an employer thinks "lactation program," he or she may imagine a dedicated pumping room with a sink and refrigerator, company-paid breast pumps, all the bells and whistles. Yet an employer can support breastfeeding in many ways. One survey of 157 U.S. businesses found that while a minority of them provided formal lactation support services, many offered the workplace flexibility that promotes breastfeeding by making the following available (Dunn, Zavela, Cline, & Cost, 2004):

- Maternity leave of three months or longer (85%)

- Flex-time, job sharing, or part-time employment options (72%)

- Breaks for expressing milk or breastfeeding (62%)

Just as breastfeeding doesn't have to be all or nothing, employers need to know that lactation support doesn't have to be all or nothing.

Mothers in School

Student mothers face many of the same issues as employed mothers, but may also have some unique hurdles. Age, type of school (high school or college), and level (secondary student, college undergraduate, graduate, post-doc) all make a difference. Sometimes both school and employment need to be addressed. For example, college or university students may attend classes, and also be paid in non-employee positions that are supported by grants or work on research projects.

In some U.S. states, Title IX can be a useful tool to work out breastfeeding accommodations. This law was passed in 1972 to ensure gender equity in educational programs that receive federal funds. Although breastfeeding isn't mentioned, it was designed to prevent discrimination against pregnant and parenting students. In 2012, the National Women's Law Center published a fact sheet addressing breastfeeding accommodations for students under Title IX (NWLC, 2012): *http://www.nwlc.org/sites/default/files/pdfs/ nwlcpregparenting_titleixfactsheet.pdf.* Any school that accepts federal funds must have a Title IX Coordinator, who can help you determine your rights.

Family Differences

Not every family is middle class and includes a husband and a wife. How can family differences affect breastfeeding? Let's look at a few examples.

Single Mothers

It's a major undertaking to raise a baby by yourself, no matter how your baby is fed, and single motherhood is becoming more common. In 2010, almost 41% of the babies born in the U.S. were born to single mothers (CDC, 2013). Breastfeeding rates vary between single and married mothers in some, but not in all studies. The takeaway message is that you need to be well-informed.

The No-Break Zone

Many employed single mothers describe their biggest challenge as their inability to take a break when feeling overwhelmed or ill. As Wendy Walsh describes in her article "Single Babe Breastfeeding: It CAN Be Done":

That tiring night (and there were more than a few) I had no one to hand her off to while I took a recharging cat-nap, no one to drive the other one to school so I wouldn't have to drag the sick one out of bed. And most of all, no one to help me with weaning. How could I distract my daughter with a different fun activity while the boobs she craved dangled in her face? (Walsh, 2011)

However, along with the challenges, there are also great rewards. Breastfeeding enhances family closeness during difficult times.

Custody Issues

For many single mothers, the baby's father isn't in the picture. When he is, custody issues may affect breastfeeding. Most courts do not consider breastfeeding a reason to prevent a father from spending time with the baby. If the father wants to be involved, during the early weeks it may help to formalize a visitation schedule of frequent, short visits that can be timed around baby's breastfeeding patterns. Ideally, overnight visits should be postponed for at least the first 3 to 4 months. At first, seeing the baby often can be more effective in forging a healthy bond than less frequent, longer visits. As baby gets older, you can supply pumped milk for longer visits. For an overview of legal and custody issues, see: *http://kellymom.com/bf/concerns/legal/bf-law/#Family*.

Low-income Mothers

Financial struggles put a tremendous strain on a family. To help offset this, most countries offer financial assistance to low-income mothers. Many government agencies also provide low-income families with free breastfeeding help. In the U.S., the government-funded Women, Infants & Children (WIC) food-subsidy program has significantly increased breastfeeding rates over the last decade. This has been a huge boon to breastfeeding, as more than half of U.S. babies born qualify for the WIC program. Many public health departments have breastfeeding specialists on hand when problems arise, and offer breast pumps for mothers returning to work, and those with babies in hospital special-care nurseries. If you are low income, find out whether you qualify for public-health benefits.

Lesbian Couples

When I ran a large private lactation practice, I learned quickly not to make assumptions about lesbian couples' breastfeeding plans. With some, only the birth mother planned to breastfeed. With others, both the birth mother and her partner planned to breastfeed. Others were adopting a baby, and one or both mothers wanted to bring in milk and breastfeed. The blog, *Gay Mom Straight World*, describes a same-sex couple who both gave birth, one to a baby boy and the other to a baby girl. One mother planned to stay home with both babies while her partner returned to work.

When induced lactation (bringing in milk without a pregnancy) is part of the plan, understanding how milk production works is key. Induced lactation works the same way as bringing in milk after birth, which is described in Chapter 3. However, expect that it will take a lot longer (a month or more) of intensive breastfeeding or pumping before much milk is produced. For induced lactation strategies that can bring in milk before baby arrives, see AskLenore. info or Alyssa Schnell's book, *Breastfeeding Without Birthing.*

Childcare

The specific childcare option you choose—day-care center, home-care setting, or a caregiver who comes to your home—is less important than the people who care for your child. You want to find people who are both good with children, and who have a caregiving style that is compatible with your own.

Childcare Questions to Ask

When you're shopping for childcare, no matter what the setting, there are some basic questions to ask.

- **What is the cost?** In-home care often costs less than a daycare center because its overhead is lower. Care in your home with a nanny, au pair, or babysitter may be higher. If a relative is providing childcare, it may be low-cost or even free.

- **How many other children do you care for and how old are they?** Adult-to-child ratio can be an important aspect of your child's quality of care.

- **How do you handle crying and feeding?** It's key that their approach be compatible with yours, even more so if it's just one person caring for your child. Do they consider crying a sign that your baby needs something? Are they willing to feed whenever baby seems hungry rather than by the clock?

- **What days and hours are you available, and what happens when I'm late?** Daycare centers usually have the strictest late policies and may charge fees for each extra minute. Although daycare centers may be open year-round, be sure to ask if they ever close. For in-home or childcare in your home, ask about vacations, snow days, school holidays, and federal holidays.

- **What back-up do you have?** One advantage of a daycare center is that if staff members are on vacation or ill, substitutes will be there. If considering an in-home arrangement, what happens in an emergency or when illness strikes?

- **What is your policy when my child is ill?** Ask about how soon your child can return once fever-free. This can make a big difference in the number of days you need to stay home from work.

- **What sort of activities are provided as my baby gets older?** Will there be social time? If your baby is cared for in your home, is the caregiver willing to go to play groups, story time, etc.? Will learning activities be available? How much of the day will be spent on screen time?

If a family member is your childcare provider, be aware that you may have less control over what happens during your baby's day. With non-family, you are the boss. Depending on the relationship, a family member may be less likely to follow your guidelines. But for a low-cost or free childcare alternative, you might be willing to accept some variance in what you consider ideal.

Childcare and Breastfeeding

Be aware of the ways your childcare choices may affect breastfeeding. Here are some aspects you may want to consider.

Distance from Work

Because more flexible access to your baby is always good for breastfeeding, consider whether it makes sense for your baby to be cared for close to your job. Having your baby nearby during your work day can make your life easier in two ways.

- At least on some days, you may have the option during your longest break of either going to baby to breastfeed or having baby brought to you. A midwork breastfeeding eliminates one pump session and gives you more baby time.

- Being nearby reduces travel time at the beginning and end of your work day, so your total time away from your baby is less, which may require less pumping at work.

I've not yet met a mother who enjoys pumping. Any strategy that cuts down on the need to pump improves quality of life. Many mothers find, too, that one breastfeeding in the middle of their work day is more effective than one pumping at maintaining milk production.

Feeding Policies and Support

With more and more mothers breastfeeding, odds are that most childcare providers have worked with breastfeeding mothers before. It can help to know, though, to what extent their policies and practices are breastfeeding friendly. (Hopefully, mothers are no longer told—as they were back in the day—that they could not bring expressed milk to daycare because it was a biohazard.) Even experienced caregivers, however, may not be fully aware of how important they are to your breastfeeding. Here are some questions to ask.

- What experience have you had in caring for a breastfeeding baby?

- How do you handle refrigerated and frozen mother's milk?

- Have you (or any of the other caregivers or their partners) breastfed?

- Do you allow mothers to breastfeed here?

As you discuss these issues, you will probably get the sense of how encouraging and supportive they are. Attitude can make a big difference.

What Your Caregiver Needs to Know About Feeding

In addition to knowing how to store and handle your milk (which is covered thoroughly in Chapter 6), if your baby is younger than 8 or 9 months old and will be bottle-fed during your work day, you may also want to encourage your caregiver to use some of the "pacing" strategies described in Chapter 8. One of the most important ways your caregiver can support your breastfeeding is by being careful not to overfeed your young baby while you're at work. Between 1 and 6 months of age, exclusively breastfed babies need on average between 25 and 30 oz. (750-900 mL) of milk per 24-hour day. If your baby gets more milk than she needs while you're at work, she won't be as interested in breastfeeding when you're together, which can cause your milk production to plummet. It also puts the pressure on you to provide much more expressed milk than necessary. Feel free to share my free online handout, "For the Caregiver of the Breastfed Baby," available at: *http://issuu. com/nancymohrbacher/docs/caregiverbfbaby.*

3

Birth and Early Breastfeeding

In previous chapters, we've covered the timing of your return to work, your job options, and how to talk to your boss about your post-baby lactation needs. Now let's focus on your birth, and priorities during your maternity leave. After devoting time to preparing for your birth, what's on your agenda afterwards? Being kind to yourself as you rest and recover is one priority. Being patient as you adjust to motherhood is another. These early postpartum weeks and months may feel like a roller coaster. But this period is key, as it sets the tone for your relationship with your baby, and lays the foundation for long-term breastfeeding. Knowing the basics will help you now and later.

Birth

Does your birth have anything to do with your return to work? It can, especially if you're going back within three months. Melissa M. from New York, USA returned to work full-time as a claims adjuster for the U.S. Department of Veterans Affairs when her son was 6 weeks and 6 days old. As she put it: "Six weeks to go through the most life and body-changing things was a pittance." As mentioned in Chapter 1, at 11 weeks postpartum many women still have childbirth-related symptoms, such as fatigue, headaches, back or neck pain, and abdominal pain (McGovern et al., 2007).

Not surprisingly, after a cesarean section, mothers report more health problems than after a vaginal birth, because they are recovering both from surgery and from having a baby. Today, many more women are having surgical deliveries. The percentages vary widely around the world. The lowest cesarean rate is 14% in the Netherlands and increases from there, with 24% in the U.K., 31% in Australia, 32% in the U.S., and a high of 47% (nearly half!) in Brazil (OECD, 2011). If your baby is born surgically, know that you're far from alone. Be extra kind and patient with yourself, and do everything possible to get extra help while you recover. Double that if your birth was traumatic psychologically, physically, or both.

One way to be kind to yourself is to take it slowly and don't try to jump right back into action. If you'll be returning to work within the first 3 months, take advantage of all offers of help and try to ease back gradually. You might find that your friends and family do not know how they can help, so you may need to ask them to do some specific things for you. Salle Webber's excellent handout, *My Friend is Going to Have a Baby: How Can I Help Her After the Birth?*, can help you get the kind of help you need. Limit visitors to supportive family and friends who will actually pitch in and help rather than expect to be waited on. If your maternity leave is longer than three months, during the first 40 days plan to stay home as much as you can, and if at all possible, arrange for help with household chores and older children. Why 40 days? Read on.

The First 40 Days

In many cultures, the first 40 days after birth are considered a special time distinct from normal life when women are cared for and their housework and childcare responsibilities are assumed by others. Among Latino societies, this time is known as *la cuarentena* (the quarantine). In China, it is known as "doing the month." Even in the U.S., where "overachiever" is our middle name, during the first half of the 20th century it was known as the "lying-in" period. Until recent decades, even American mothers received round-the-clock care and support during the first weeks after giving birth. Postpartum help aids in the physical recovery from childbirth, but the first 40 days are also a time of intense breastfeeding and having help can make the usual feeding frenzies much easier to handle.

To understand what to expect and why breastfeeding is so intense during the early weeks, you need to know how milk production works and how this breastfeeding intensity relates to your supply and your baby's needs. But before discussing milk-making in more depth, let's look at some dynamics unique to this time and how they may affect your priorities.

Timing Is Everything

Do you wonder (like many) if you should devote your maternity leave to getting your baby used to the bottle and establishing the feeding routines you expect later? Many mothers understandably want to do everything possible to make their return to work easier on their baby. Consciously or subconsciously, some even worry about allowing themselves to get too close to their newborn for fear it may be too hard to leave him when the time comes. If you're feeling pressured now to try to prepare yourself and your baby for your separations later, take a deep breath and consider another point of view. This kind of advance preparation may take you in the opposite direction from where you want to go.

"What might be a great strategy at 4 months can be a total disaster at 1 week. For that reason, it helps to understand and take full advantage of the unique dynamics of each stage."

Why? Because timing is everything. Different strategies work best at different ages and stages.

The amount of milk you produce, your body's responsiveness to breast stimulation, and your baby's needs and adaptability all change over time. What might be a great strategy at 4 months can be a total disaster at 1 week. For that reason, it helps to understand and take full advantage of the unique dynamics of each stage. By planning accordingly, not only will everyone be happier, but it will also be easier to meet your long-term goals. What you do now affects what happens later.

Start by thinking of your maternity leave as a unique bubble of time with your top priority to forge a strong, loving bond with your baby. You have plenty of time later to pump and bottle-feed. (You'll soon read some tips for this.) In fact, almost no one enjoys pumping and bottle-feeding. The time you can focus on just you and your baby is the best part. Don't miss it! Give yourself permission now to get in sync with your newborn. That will strengthen your all-important connection and build a milk supply that will carry you through whatever timeframe you have in mind. By being responsive to your baby's hunger cues, and doing lots of holding and cuddling, you will make the most of this "babymoon." Now on to the nitty-gritty.

How Milk Production Works

During the first 2 weeks after birth, your body is more responsive to breast stimulation than at any other time in your life. The hormones of childbirth prepare your body to produce milk abundantly. In fact, practically speaking, the sky's the limit. Amazingly, by just breastfeeding whenever your baby shows signs of hunger (rooting, hand-to-mouth, fussing), mothers of multiples have produced enough milk for twins, triplets, quadruplets, even quintuplets. During that incredible first two weeks, your body is just waiting for you to tell it how much milk to make. To communicate this, though, you need to know how to speak your body's language.

The Language of Milk Removals

The language your body understands is conveyed through milk removals. The more often and more fully your breasts are drained of milk, the more milk you produce. The less often and less fully the milk is removed, the less milk you produce. Simply put, drained breasts make milk faster, and full breasts make milk slower.

Two aspects of full breasts slow milk production: 1) internal pressure as your breasts fill with milk, and 2) an ingredient in your milk known as feedback inhibitor of lactation, or FIL. As more milk accumulates in your breasts, increasing pressure and FIL send a signal to your breasts to slow milk production. The more pressure and FIL in your breasts, the stronger the signal. The fuller your breasts become, the slower you make milk (Kent, Prime, & Garbin, 2011).

The opposite is also true. Milk production speeds when your milk is removed more often and more fully. When a growing baby starts to need more milk, he feeds more times per day and for longer stretches, taking more of the milk available in your breasts. Table 3-1 shows how baby's average milk intake increases during the first 6 months.

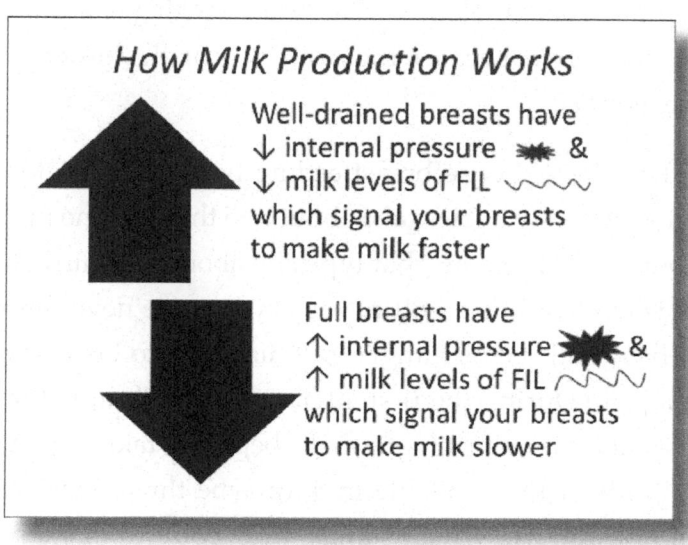

How Milk Production Works

Well-drained breasts have
↓ internal pressure ⚬ &
↓ milk levels of FIL 〰
which signal your breasts
to make milk faster

Full breasts have
↑ internal pressure ✦ &
↑ milk levels of FIL 〰
which signal your breasts
to make milk slower

Baby's Age	Average volume per feeding	Average volume per day
1 day	0.2 oz. (10 mL)	2 oz. (50 mL)
3 days	1 oz. (30 mL)	8 oz. (250 mL)
1 week	1.5 oz. (45 mL)	15 oz. (450 mL)
2 weeks	2 oz. (60 mL)	20 oz. (600 mL)
1 month	3-4 oz. (90-120 mL)	25-30 oz. (750-900 mL)
6 months	3-4 oz. (90-120 mL)	30 oz. (900 mL)

Table 3-1. *Baby's average feeding volume by age.*

Notice that almost all of the increase in milk intake occurs during the first month or so. That's why early breastfeeding is so much more intense then than it will be later. Unlike formula-fed babies, breastfed babies consume about the same amount of milk per day at 1 month as they do at around 6 months (Kent et al., 2013). Yet they continue to grow and thrive, because their rate of growth slows during those months.

How does intense breastfeeding boost your milk production? Usually babies take about two thirds of the milk in the breasts. This means that typically about one third of the milk is left. (Unlike a bottle, your breasts are never empty, so if baby still seems hungry, put him back to breast again and again.) During the first 40 days, as baby's appetite increases and his stomach grows, he begins to take more than two thirds of the available milk (maybe three quarters or even nine tenths), which signals your body to make more milk faster. You always produce more than your baby actually needs, and if he takes more of the extra milk, this tells your body to speed milk production.

This natural system, however, only works as it's supposed to if you breastfeed whenever baby seems hungry rather than on a schedule. At this stage, giving a pacifier regularly can throw this system off, too, because it delays feedings. If the pacifier is given often, this can mean fewer feedings per day, which sends the signal to produce less milk. Giving regular bottles of formula has the same effect. If a baby is not gaining weight well, giving expressed milk or formula can sometimes be necessary. But if your baby is doing well without it, giving formula regularly can undermine your long-term goals by limiting your milk production.

Just to clarify, the first 2 weeks are not the only time you can increase your milk production. It can be done at any stage. Even women who have never been pregnant have produced milk for adopted babies by simply breastfeeding or pumping often. What you need to know is that during the first 2 weeks, bringing your milk production to "full" is easier now than it will ever be again. Your postpartum hormonal levels help get your milk production where you want it for the long term with the least amount of work. Boosting your milk supply takes much less time and effort now than it will later.

There's another reason that it makes sense to make the most of this first 40 days to get to full production quickly. With full production and a more mature baby, breastfeeding becomes much less intense and time consuming. With practice and growth, babies finish feeding in a shorter time. With larger stomachs, they can take more milk and stay content longer with fewer feeds per day. Early breastfeeding can feel overwhelming—something like a marathon—but sticking with it and getting to the "reward period" that starts at around 6 weeks is well worth it. Over the long run, this early investment pays you back many times over in time, cost-savings, and better health for you and your baby.

Breast Storage Capacity

This second major milk-production dynamic is useful to know about now, but is even more important later. The language of milk removals is universal. But feeding patterns among mothers and babies vary a lot, in part because of this physical difference. Understanding breast storage capacity is key to understanding milk production in both the short and long term.

Breast storage capacity is determined by the volume of milk available in your breasts at their fullest time of the day. Storage capacity is not related to breast size, which is determined mostly by how much fatty tissue is in your breasts. Smaller-breasted mothers can have a large storage capacity and larger-breasted mothers can have a small capacity. Storage capacity varies by how much room is in your milk-making glands.

How do differences in storage capacity affect breast-feeding? Not much at first, when baby's stomach is so small. But after baby's stomach grows larger, a mother with a large storage capacity will likely notice a very different breast-feeding pattern than a mother with a small storage capacity. Storage capacity may affect feedings in several ways.

- Whether your baby usually takes one breast or both.

- Number of feedings needed each day for your baby to gain weight

- Your baby's longest sleep stretch

Both large-capacity and small-capacity mothers produce plenty of milk. Their babies simply feed differently to get the milk they need. What matters to babies is not how much milk they get per feeding, but how much milk they get in a 24-hour day.

A mother with a large storage capacity has more room in her breasts to hold milk. Because she has more room, in order for there to be enough internal pressure to slow milk production, more milk must accumulate. With so much milk available in her breasts, her baby may always be satisfied with one breast per feeding. He may gain weight well with fewer feedings per day than most babies. And he may sleep for longer stretches at night without her milk production slowing.

The mother with a small storage capacity, on the other hand, will have less milk available at each feeding. For this reason, her baby may want both breasts more often, need more feedings each day to get the same amount of milk, and need to continue night feedings longer. If the baby of the small-capacity mother sleeps for too long, her breasts quickly become so full that milk production slows.

Think of storage capacity as being on a spectrum from very large to very small and every point in between. When you return to work, figuring out where you fall on this spectrum will allow you to customize your daily routine. See Chapters 9 and 11 for details.

Your Baby's Needs and Ability to Adapt

Your baby obviously also plays a major role in how early breastfeeding goes. To understand this better, let's start at the beginning. While in the womb, your baby never felt hunger. He was fed constantly by the nutrients flowing through the umbilical cord. After birth, he feels hunger for the first time. Digesting milk in his stomach and experiencing hunger pangs between feedings are new experiences. To make this transition easier, your breasts start by producing small amounts of milk. Milk production increases over time with frequent nursing.

At birth, small feedings are better for your baby than larger feedings because your newborn's stomach is tiny. An average feeding on the first day of life is about one third of an ounce (10 mL) of colostrum, the early milk you've been making since mid-pregnancy. Colostrum provides concentrated nutrition in amounts perfectly sized to your baby's tiny tummy. With frequent breastfeeding during the first week, your milk production increases every day. As your baby takes more milk per feeding, his stomach gently expands. By his third day, his stomach comfortably holds about an ounce (30 mL) of milk. Your baby's stomach size and your milk production both affect early feeding patterns. Take another look at Table 3-1 to review the big increase in your milk production during the first month of life.

Attempts to schedule your baby's feedings by the clock during these early weeks are likely to move you further away from your breastfeeding goals. Why? Your baby's stomach is too small to hold enough milk to keep him regularly content for long periods. If feedings are on a schedule, because of baby's small stomach, he will likely spend some parts of the day hungry and crying, which is stressful for everyone. Also, longer intervals between feedings mean fewer daily milk removals, which will prevent the increases in milk production that are key to meeting your long-term goals. If milk is removed fewer times per day, your body will get the message that you don't need more milk.

After 40 days or so, your baby's stomach will have grown bigger, your milk production will be at its peak, and for many babies a more predictable feeding pattern occurs naturally. Trying to make that happen before its natural time is likely to make life harder for everyone. Also, as your baby matures, he becomes more adaptable to change. Waiting until he's older to make adjustments in his feeding pattern will increase the odds that he can handle them well.

What Breastfeeding Norms Look Like

What should you expect breastfeeding to be like during these first 40 days? When it is going normally, small feedings often mean periods of very frequent and sometimes nonstop nursing. Unlike many babies fed by bottle, most breastfed newborns do not feed at regular time intervals. While it is true that most young babies breastfeed 8 to 12 times every 24 hours, the usual laws of math simply don't apply here.

Cluster Feeding

During the first 40 days or so, your baby probably won't have any sort of regular feeding pattern. This means tracking feedings closely (i.e., number of minutes per breast) provides no real benefit. Most new babies tend to bunch their feedings together at certain times (called cluster nursing), and go longer between feedings at other times. If you're lucky, these longer stretches (up to 4 to 5 hours is fine) will be at night. But don't get your hopes up. At first, because most babies are born with their days and nights mixed up, these longer stretches will probably be during the day.

Your baby wanting to breastfeed soon after a feeding is not a sign that your milk production is low; it's a sign that your baby is doing a good job of bringing in abundant milk.

What's Your Focus?

You'll probably hear all sorts of recommendations about how long to breastfeed, whether to give one or both breasts, how long is "long enough" to feed on one breast. And how conflicting advice about these sorts of things can be crazy-making, and there are a hundred different baby tracking apps available that record all sorts of information, but give you no context in which to put it.

The truth is that when it comes to early breastfeeding, the clock is not your friend. Why isn't timing important? Because just like grownups, breastfed babies can be fast or slow eaters. Two different babies can consume the same

Figure 3-1. *When it comes to early breastfeeding, the clock is not your friend.*

amount of milk in vastly different time frames, from 5 minutes to 45 minutes. It's not helpful to track or even to care how long or how often your baby breastfeeds.

So what *do* you focus on? If this is your first breastfed baby, you may wonder how to know whether breastfeeding is going well. It's good to keep an eye on three things during the first couple of weeks. One is your baby's weight, which is the most reliable way to know how breastfeeding is going. After reaching their low weight on day 3 or 4, breastfed babies gain on average about 1 oz. (30 mL) per day during their first three months. Between weight checks, it's a good idea to keep track of:

- Number of feedings per day (a feeding can mean taking one or both breasts)

- Number of poops

You're looking for a minimum of eight feedings in a 24-hour day. After your baby's poop turns yellow (usually by day 4 or 5), you should expect to see at least three to four poops the size of a U.S. quarter (22 mm) or larger. Your baby's poops are formed from the fatty hindmilk he needs to put on weight. So if you see at least three to four poops per day, you don't need to worry about number of wet diapers. Because the hindmilk comes after the watery foremilk during feedings, if your baby has the right number of poops, you can assume your baby received plenty of fluids. With both number of feedings and number of poops, you can have too few (and if you do, it's time to arrange for a weight check), but you can't have too many.

Rather than timing breastfeeding by the clock, when all is going well, the recommended feeding strategy is called "finish the first breast first." This means letting your baby breastfeed as long as he likes on the first breast. When he comes off or falls asleep and falls off, offer the other breast. Typically, babies take one breast at some feedings and both breasts at some feedings. By leaving this up to your baby, you can be sure he will get the right amount of milk and will be able to adjust your supply as needed. If your baby is done after one breast, give the other breast at the next feeding. (If baby is clustering feedings together, begin counting the next feeding after at least a 30-minute gap.)

Being back up to birth weight by his 2-week checkup or gaining about an ounce (30 g) per day means your baby is an effective feeder. Once he's proven himself, you don't need to keep track of feedings. Just follow your baby's lead.

Day and Night

What should you expect during the early weeks in terms of feeding patterns? If your baby is typical, feedings will vary by time of day. One of the many differences between breast and bottle is that a breast is not like a faucet, with the milk at the same level day and night. Your milk has its own natural ebb and flow, which affects how your baby's feeds.

During mornings, milk production is usually at its peak. Mothers often report that their babies go longer between feedings in the morning than in the evening, when milk production is at its lowest ebb. Babies get the milk they need in the evening by feeding more often, every hour or even every half hour. This is a completely normal pattern and it does not mean that your milk production is low.

These evening breastfeeding marathons are usually confined to the first 40 days. With growth, your baby's stomach gets bigger and he can hold more milk. And with practice at the breast, your baby learns to get more milk more quickly. With time, your breastfeeding pattern will change, usually becoming more predictable. What's important about this for your baby is not the ebb and flow; it's the total amount of milk he gets every 24 hours.

What About Pumping and Storing?

The early weeks are not the best time to start pumping to store milk. But there are sometimes good reasons to pump now.

Not the Best Time to Store Milk

Why are the first 40 days not the best time to store milk? Review Table 3-1 again. If your pumping experience is average and you pump between regular feedings, your milk yield will be about half a feeding. If you pump instead of breastfeeding at a usual feeding time, expect to pump a full feeding. At about 1 week, half a feeding is a paltry 0.75 oz. (22.5 mL) of milk. Unless you have a specific reason for providing your baby with extra milk during this time, it is hardly worth the time and effort. (Don't forget, after pumping you still have to clean the pump parts!) Some women who pump early and get average amounts assume wrongly that there's something amiss with their milk production. Even if you know the averages, it's still pretty discouraging. If you wait to start pumping and storing until your milk production increases, you'll get much more milk for your efforts. (For more on realistic expectations, see Chapter 5.)

What are good reasons to pump? Imagine that your newborn nurses really well from one breast but then is sound asleep and not willing to take the other, very full breast. What do you do? You've basically got two choices. You can express your milk or you can leave your very full breast as is until the next feeding. Allowing your breast to stay overly full for long stretches is not a good plan, because it can lead to a painful condition called mastitis. (For details, see the next section.) This is definitely not something you want. Most women experience this as a sore area or lump in one breast, and it can lead to a fever and chills. Any time your breast is full and your baby is not willing to breast-feed, pumping some milk can both keep you comfortable and prevent mastitis from developing, both good things.

One word of caution here. As mentioned, your breasts are much more sensitive to stimulation during the first 2 weeks than they will be at any other time in your life. This means you don't want to overdo it. When mothers do a lot of pumping now, it can lead to oversupply, which means producing much more milk than your baby needs. If you will not be pumping at work and you want to accumulate a huge reserve of milk during maternity leave, lots of pumping now might make sense. If that isn't your situation, there are serious downsides of oversupply for both for you and for your baby. There can definitely be too much of a good thing!

For your baby, a drawback of oversupply is a very fast milk flow. Even without oversupply, it's not uncommon during the first few weeks for babies to sometimes cough, sputter, and pull away from the breast when milk flow becomes overwhelming. But with an oversupply, this can be a constant challenge that leads to unhappiness and breast-feeding struggles.

For you, the drawbacks of oversupply include the possibility that your baby may start clamping down on your nipple during feedings to prevent too-fast milk flow. When you produce much more milk than your baby consumes, this also means that for some parts of the day, your breasts may feel uncomfortably full, which is unpleasant. Staying full for too long can lead to mastitis, described later. To relieve this fullness and prevent mastitis, you may need to pump often, which is another drawback, as pumping is extra work for you and not exactly fun. Depending on how you pump, this may either be part of the problem or part of the solution.

How do you pump to keep yourself comfortable without causing oversupply? It's actually not hard. You use a strategy called "pump to comfort." This means whenever you feel full and your baby is not willing to nurse, you just pump long enough for your breast to feel okay, but not long enough to fully drain it. This might take one minute, three minutes, five minutes, or more. The key is that you stop pumping as soon as you feel comfortable. Draining your breasts fully many times each day can lead to oversupply. Pumping to comfort during the early weeks has no drawbacks other than the work involved. It allows your milk production to adjust to the right level without risk of pain or mastitis, and you can store any milk you pump.

FAQ: Common Early Problems

Hopefully, you won't have the following early breastfeeding challenges, but if you do, here are some fundamentals as a starting point. For more details, you may want to have a basic breastfeeding book on hand, such as *Breastfeeding Made Simple* or *Breastfeeding Solutions*. Another more portable option is the *Breastfeeding Solutions* smartphone app. Links to download it onto Android and iPhones are at: *http://www.nancymohrbacher.com/app-support* .

Nipple Pain

The most important thing to know about nipple pain is that it is a fixable problem. It's not something you just have to live with.

How much nipple pain is normal during early breastfeeding?

Anything more than mild discomfort during the first minute or two of feedings during the first week or two is a sign that your pain is outside the normal range. Toe-curling pain, pain throughout the feeding, skin trauma or color changes are all signs that it's time to make adjustments. If your own adjustments aren't enough to make breastfeeding comfortable, seek help. Needing breastfeeding help is not a commentary on your mothering skills; a small tweak in how your baby latches is usually all that's needed. Even if someone has already told you that your latch "looks fine," how it looks is not what's important. What matters is how it feels.

What's the connection between baby's latch and sore nipples?

The deeper your nipple extends into your baby's mouth during feedings, the more comfortable breastfeeding should feel. To gauge how deep is deep enough, run your tongue or your finger along the roof of your mouth. The section nearest your front teeth is ridged. Behind these ridges is a smooth area, your hard palate. Closer to your throat, the roof of your mouth becomes soft. The area nicknamed the "comfort zone" is near that part of your baby's mouth where his palate turns from hard to soft. Reaching the comfort zone during breastfeeding protects your nipple from friction and pressure, and your baby gets more milk with each suck.

If your baby latches shallowly, his tongue compresses your nipple against his hard palate, causing nipple distortion and pain. Your nipple may come out of your baby's mouth oddly shaped, smashed looking, or pointed. If your baby breastfeeds with a shallow latch feeding after feeding, this may eventually lead to pain, skin trauma, and bleeding.

How can I get a deeper latch?

Latching a newborn can feel complicated if you're sitting up or lying on your side because gravity pulls your baby down and away from you. Many mothers find that using more relaxed, or laid-back, breastfeeding positions (a term coined by U.K. researcher Suzanne Colson) can make getting a deep latch easier and more automatic during the early weeks. In these positions, gravity works in harmony with your baby's inborn feeding behaviors.

To do this, lean back far enough so baby's entire weight rests tummy down on your body, but upright enough so that you can see him easily without straining your neck. Think of you and your baby as two puzzle pieces. While experimenting, use these two adjustments to help you find your best fit:

1. **How far you lean back.** Experiment until you find an angle that works for you. Some mothers like their head and shoulders higher or lower.

2. **From which direction your baby approaches the breast.** Put your baby lengthwise, diagonally, or across your torso until you find a position he likes (Figures 3-2, 3-3, & 3-4).

When you lay your baby tummy down near your exposed breasts, your baby's inborn feeding behaviors are triggered and he may bob his way to the breast. If he seems to need your help, feel free to give it. Nature hardwires babies to get to the breast and feed in these more natural positions. When your baby's feeding behaviors are triggered and he has an active role in taking the breast, many mothers find they achieve an even deeper latch than when they try to micromanage it while in a sitting-straight-up position.

Figures 3-2, 3-3, and 3-4. *Several laid-back breastfeeding positions to try.* ©2014 Anna Mohrbacher. Used with permission.

You'll know you have a deeper latch when breastfeeding feels more comfortable than before. If you have nipple trauma, breastfeeding may not yet feel completely comfortable. Any reduction in pain indicates you've reached the comfort zone. By getting your nipple into the comfort zone at every breastfeeding, your nipples can heal even while continuing to breastfeed.

Are there other causes of nipple pain?

Yes. One easy-to-correct cause is not breaking your baby's suction first when you take your baby off the breast. Another is having your pump suction up too high or using a pump with a too-small nipple tunnel (see Chapter 4). Overzealous cleaning of your nipples or the use harsh products can also cause soreness. Another cause is lack of blood flow to the nipple, which can be due to circulatory problems. (If this is the cause, when the pain starts, your nipple will turn white, blue, or red.) Some babies are tongue-tied, which can also cause nipple soreness, even with a deep latch. A lactation consultant should be able to check your baby for this anatomical variation. You can read more about tongue tie in this online article: *https://breastfeedingusa.org/content/article/tell-me-about-tongue-ties.* Other causes of pain include infected nipples or a clogged nipple pore (white spot on the nipple).

What should I do if I can't get comfortable?

If you have tried getting a deeper latch on your own and you're still in pain, it's time to seek skilled breastfeeding help. You can find a board-certified lactation consultant in your area by going to the website, *www.ilca.org,* click on its "Find a Lactation Consultant" page, and enter your ZIP or postal code.

Some products, such as ultrapurified lanolin and hydrogel pads, can be soothing when you're sore, but unless you correct the cause of the problem, they will only help temporarily.

Engorgement

Engorgement is not an inevitable part of early breastfeeding. Severe engorgement usually only happens when your baby does not breastfeed often or effectively in the early days.

How will I know if I have engorgement?

When it happens, engorgement usually starts around the third or fourth day after birth. Most mothers feel breast fullness around this time, but if your breasts are very full, very firm, painful, hard, or hot, you may be engorged. Engorgement is not just caused by an increase in your milk production. Other body fluids, such as extra blood and lymph, are also drawn to your breasts as your milk production ramps up, contributing to congestion there.

Engorgement can make the area around your nipple (areola) firm, making a deep latch difficult, and sometimes causing the nipple to flatten. To get a deep latch, the areola must be soft enough to change shape during suckling, so the nipple can extend into the "comfort zone."

What's the best way to treat engorgement?

When engorged, many mothers worry about breastfeeding more often and expressing milk, because they're concerned they may make it worse. But the best thing you can do to relieve engorgement is to drain your breasts often and well. Try these treatments.

- **Breastfeed your baby at least 8 to 12 times a day** (more is better), every 1.5 to 2 hours during the day and 2 to 3 hours at night until you feel relief. Make sure your baby has a deep latch.

- **If a deep latch is difficult, use reverse pressure softening** to move the swelling away from your nipples. This simple technique was developed by K. Jean Cotterman, RNC, IBCLC. You can see a video demonstration at: *http://on.aol.com/video/how-to-use-reverse-pressure-softening-during-engorgement-106182017*

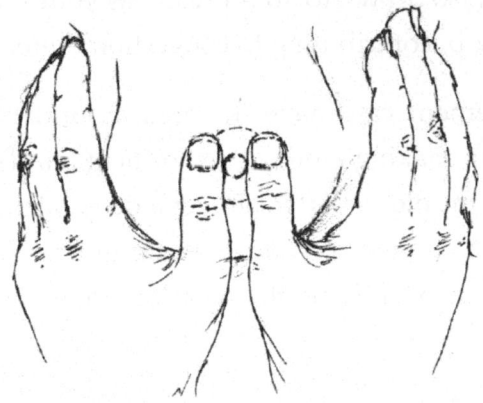

Figure 3-5. *Reverse pressure softening can move the swelling back into your breast to make it easier to get a deep latch.* ©2014 Kyle Cotterman. Used with permission.

- **If your baby is not breastfeeding well or at all, use an effective breast pump** to drain your breasts well at least eight times per day.

- **Avoid bottles, pacifiers, or formula supplements** to keep baby at the breast.

- **Apply warmth before feedings to aid milk flow and cool between feedings to reduce swelling.**

- **Take an anti-inflammatory medication,** such as ibuprofen. Ask your health care provider to recommend one.

- **Wear a supportive bra** that fits you well and is not too tight.

If you follow the above suggestions, your symptoms should begin to clear within a day or two. If they don't, contact a breastfeeding specialist.

Mastitis

About one in five breastfeeding mothers develops mastitis at some point, so if you develop this condition, know that you're not alone.

What is mastitis?

Mastitis refers to an inflammation of the breast, with or without a fever. A mild form of mastitis—a tender spot or lump in your breast with no fever—is sometimes referred to as a plugged, clogged, or blocked duct. If you have a temperature of more than 101°F (38.4°C), are achy, or have other symptoms that feel like the flu, you probably have a more severe case that has progressed into an infection. Other signs of infection include a cracked nipple with pus, pus or blood in your milk, red streaks on your breast, and severe symptoms that appear suddenly.

How can I treat mastitis?

For mastitis with and without infection, the treatment is generally the same. However, if you think you have an infection, call your health care provider and ask about a prescription of antibiotics, and then follow the suggestions below.

- **Breastfeed frequently on the affected breast**. Drain that breast often by breastfeeding or pumping. Letting milk accumulate in your breast will make it worse. If breastfeeding is uncomfortable, use whichever positions are most comfortable. If your baby refuses to nurse on your affected side, pump until the infection heals.

- **Ask your health care provider about using a pain reliever, such as ibuprofen.**

- **Apply heat to the area and gently massage it** from your armpit to your nipple. Use warm compresses at least 3 times a day.

- **Breastfeed your baby right after the heat treatment** to help loosen the plug.

- **Wear loose clothing.** Consider whether your bra might be too tight, which is one possible cause of mastitis.

- **Rest.** This enhances your body's natural defenses.

What causes mastitis?

One key to avoiding mastitis in the future is to determine why you got it in the first place. These are the most common causes.

- Nipple trauma, which lets organisms enter the breast

- Consistent pressure on your breast for long periods, such as from a bra that's too tight, a strap that cuts across your chest, or sleeping on your stomach

- Prolonged breast fullness from irregular feeding patterns or suddenly going longer between feedings (your baby sleeping through the night, busy holidays, the use of supplements or a pacifier). If you can determine the cause, you may be able to prevent mastitis from occurring again.

See the Resources section for how to find skilled breastfeeding help in your area when needed.

4

Breast Pump Choice and Fit

If you've never used a breast pump, the whole idea of pumping your milk may seem strange and even off-putting. If you plan to use a pump, learning a little about it may help you feel more at ease. But before getting into these specifics, know up front that like breastfeeding, pumping is not supposed to hurt. A key part of comfortable pumping is choosing a pump that's right for your situation and one that fits you well, which this chapter explains in more detail.

Your Situation and Pump Choice

If you plan to use a breast pump, the first step is deciding which type of pump to get. It's easy to feel confused by the large array of breast pumps online and on store shelves. Knowing which type of pump is better suited to which situations may narrow your choices and make this process easier. How often you plan to pump, and your reason for pumping, can help you decide on the best pump for you. Below are some common reasons why women need a pump.

Your Newborn Isn't Breastfeeding or Your Supply Needs a Boost

The recommended pumps in these situations are those used in hospitals. You will probably rent this type of pump, and the pump motor is shared. Each mother buys her own milk collection kit (the parts that comes into contact with the milk), so one mother's milk never touches another's. A double milk-collection kit lets you pump both breasts at the same time (double pumping), which takes half the time of pumping one breast at a time (single pumping). These pumps (Figure 4-1) are larger and heavier than those purchased for home or office use, because they are made to be durable enough to be used by many women. See the Resources section for website URLs of the three major brands

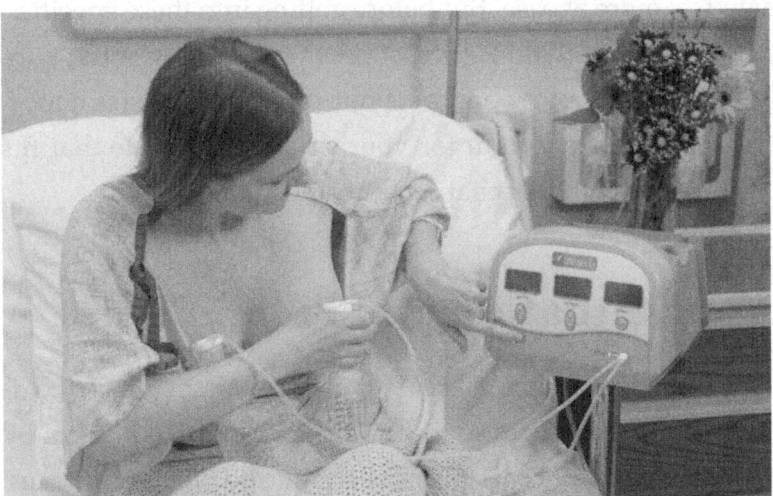

Figure 4-1. *This mother, who is pumping in the hospital for a premature baby, uses one arm to double pump so she has a hand free to adjust her rental pump's controls.* ©2014 Ameda, Inc. Used with permission.

of rental pumps: Ameda, Hygeia, and Medela. You can find the closest pump rental business near you online.

Some of these pumps provide slightly stronger suction than the pumps you can buy, but that's not why they're recommended. Most provide a smoother feel, and more suction and speed settings. These differences make them the best choice when a baby is not nursing at all or when milk production needs a boost.

You'll Be Working Full-Time or Pumping Daily

If you'll be pumping once a day or more often, consider buying a double-electric breast pump with a motor warranty of at least one year. (Those with shorter warranties may not be durable enough to meet your needs.) These pumps are sometimes called "professional grade," and are not recommended for sharing, because their motors are not heavy-duty enough to work properly after multiple users (see Figure 4-2). Some brands are not safe to share for hygiene reasons (see later section on used breast pumps).

These pumps come with a double milk-collection kit so pumping takes half the time of single pumping. Whatever your work setting, if you'll be doing a lot of pumping, the total time spent is important. These pumps are available with or without carry bags. Pump bag styles include shoulder bags and backpacks, and all bags include an insulated cooling compartment for milk storage during the work day.

Most have battery options. Recommended brands include Ameda, Hygeia, and Medela (see the Resources section). Different mothers respond differently to the "feels" of various breast pump models (Kent, Ramsay, Doherty, Larsson, & Hartmann, 2003). That means there's not one pump make and model that works best for everyone

Some women get more milk per session with a manual pump than with an electric double pump, but because manual pumps require more muscle power, using them daily may not be practical long-term. If this is true for you, try the hands-on pumping technique described in the next chapter with an electric pump to increase your milk yield.

Figure 4-2. *Professional-grade pumps are smaller and lighter than rental pumps. Most have battery options, carry bags, and compartments to store and cool milk.* ©2014 Hygeia. Used with permission.

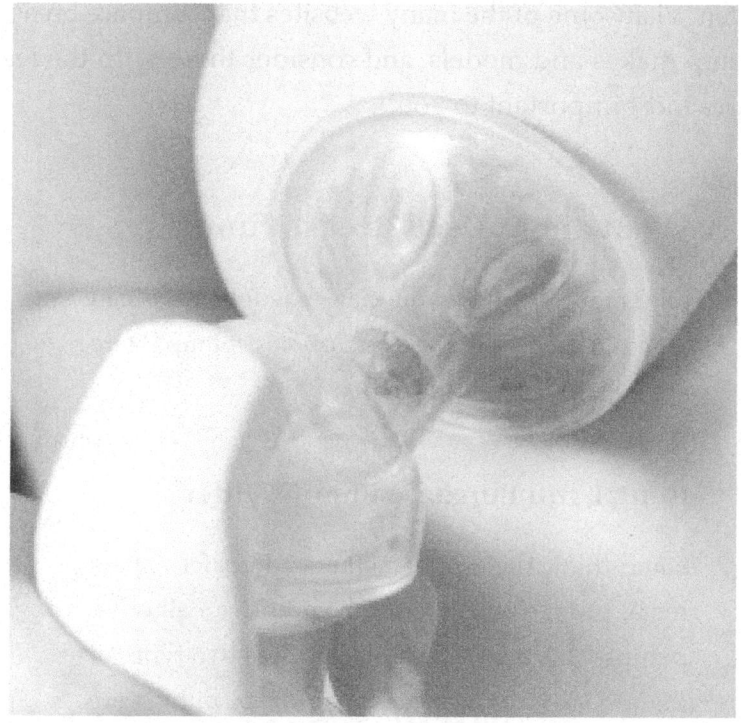

Figure 4-3. *A manual pump requires muscle power to operate. It may be a good choice if you're not planning to pump every day.*

You'll Be Working PartTime or Not Pumping Daily

If you work less than 20 hours per week, or you'll be breastfeeding your baby during your work day, you will not be relying as heavily on your breast pump to establish or maintain your milk production. This gives you many more options. Keep in mind that if you buy a single pump, pumping one breast at a time takes twice as long as double pumping. A manual pump, which is usually powered by squeezing the pump's handle, can get tiring if you use it often. Visit some of the many websites that compare breast-pump makes and models, and consider those with the features most important to you.

What about Used Breast Pumps?

Like many women, you may wonder if you can save money by getting a used breast pump. Here are the main points to ponder.

Rental and Purchase Pumps Differ

Some think that since mothers can safely share rental pumps, it is safe for them to share all other pumps. This is not true because these two types of pumps have different designs. Rental pumps are designed so your milk never touches the working parts of the pump that are shared with other mothers. The inner workings of most purchase pumps come in contact with milk particles during pumping, and there is no surefire way to avoid mixing milk.

Hygiene Issues

If you buy, borrow, or are given a used purchase pump, in most cases, it's impossible to prevent other mothers' milk particles from being blown into your milk during pumping. This is why some compare pumping with a used breast pump to sharing someone else's toothbrush.

With Medela double-electric purchase pumps, for example, the pump piece held against your breast is open to the pump's tubing, which is also open to the piece over the pump motor that generates the suction and release. This means that an invisible mist of milk particles can travel through the tubing to the inside of the pump. The piece inside the pump that the milk particles touch cannot be removed or sterilized, so it cannot be cleaned well enough between mothers to ensure safety—even with a new set of bottles and tubing. You may not see these milk particles, but they are the reason that mold sometimes grows in pump tubing. In contrast, Ameda's electric pumps are designed with a solid barrier between the milk and the pump tubing.

Wear and Tear

Another key consideration is whether a used pump will work well. Most rental pumps are bigger, heavier, and more durable than purchase pumps, which were designed to be used by one person only. Better double-electric purchase pumps have a one-year warranty on their motor, compared with a three-year warranty on most rental pumps.

If someone loans you her double-electric purchase pump, keep in mind that you will reduce its lifespan by however long you use it. Even if the original owner doesn't want the pump back, you have no way of knowing if it is still in good working order. If pumping is key to your milk production, starting with a new pump is a wise investment.

Pump Fit

If you'll be doing a lot of pumping, you'll want this time to be both productive and comfortable. Pump fit is key to both.

What Determines Pump Fit?

Pump fit is not about breast size; it's about nipple size. It refers to how well your nipples fit into the pump opening or "nipple tunnel" (Figure 4-4) that your nipple is pulled into during pumping.

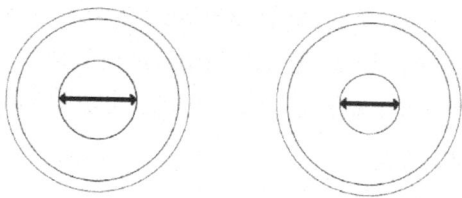

Figure 4-4. *Pump nipple tunnels come in different sizes.* ©2014 Anna Mohrbacher. Used with permission.

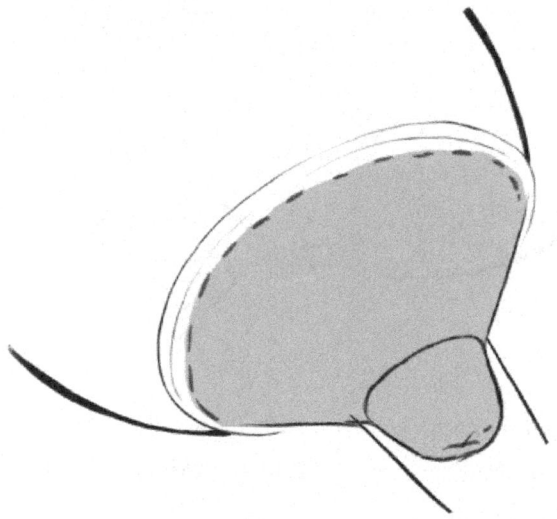

Figure 4-5. *A good fit means having some space around your entire nipple during pumping.* ©2014 Anna Mohrbacher. Used with permission.

You'll know you have a good pump fit if you see some (but not too much) space around your nipple as it moves freely in and out of the nipple tunnel (Figure 4-5).

If any part of your nipple rubs along the tunnel's sides, it is too small (Figure 4-6). It can also be too large. Ideally, you want no more than about a quarter inch (6 mm) of the dark circle around your nipple (areola) pulled into the tunnel during pumping.

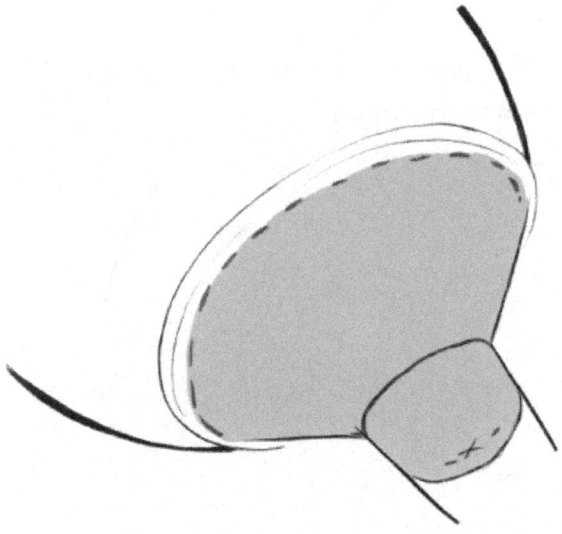

Figure 4-6. *Your nipple tunnel is too small if any part of your nipple rubs against it.* ©2014 Anna Mohrbacher. Used with permission.

Too much areola pulled into the tunnel can cause rubbing and soreness (Figure 4-7). You'll know you probably need a different size nipple tunnel if you feel discomfort during pumping, even when your pump's suction control is near its lowest setting.

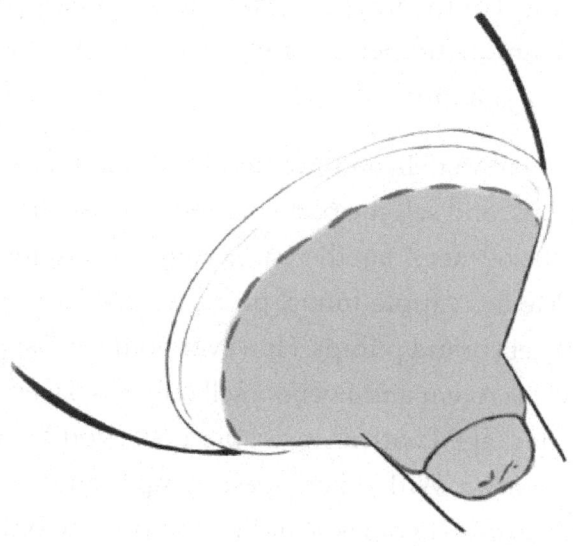

Figure 4-7. *Your nipple tunnel is too large if too much areola is pulled in and rubs.* ©2014 Anna Mohrbacher. Used with permission.

A good fit is important because it affects both your comfort and milk flow (Jones & Hilton, 2009). If the nipple tunnel squeezes your nipple during pumping, this slows your milk flow and you pump less milk. Either a too-large or too-small nipple tunnel can cause discomfort and stress, both of which also slow milk flow.

Available Sizes

Before getting a breast pump, find out how many size options the brand you're considering offers. If the only size option is the one that comes with the pump, you're taking a chance. Most companies that make quality breast pumps sell several nipple-tunnel sizes so that you can fit your pump to your anatomy.

The popular Medela and Ameda brands offer six or seven size options, and sell the part with the nipple tunnel separately, so if you need another size, you can buy just that piece. The Medela nipple-tunnel pieces are also compatible with the Hygeia brand pumps. However, some breast pump brands, such as Avent and Evenflo, sell only two sizes. Their pumps are packaged with an insert piece that you can either leave in or remove. With other breast pump brands, such as Playtex, the size that comes with the pump is the only size available.

Confused about where to start? Even before birth, you can use common objects to gauge which nipple-tunnel size you may want to try first. For example, hold a U.S. nickel up to your nipple. (If you live elsewhere, use any coin with a 22.5 mm diameter.) If your nipple width is larger than this, start with the next size up from standard. If your nipple is as wide as a U.S. quarter (25 mm) or larger, you may want to start with two sizes up from standard. On the other hand, if your nipple is smaller than a nickel (22.5 mm), start with the standard size that comes with the pump. However, if your nipple is quite a bit smaller than the nickel (perhaps the size of a pencil eraser), start with a smaller-than-standard size.

Because your nipples may vary in size, you may get better pumping results if you use a different nipple-tunnel size for each breast. The only way to know if the size you're using is the best fit for you is to experiment with several sizes. Some pumps come with multiple size options.

Pump Fit Changes Over Time

Once you find your best pump fit, that's not the end of the story. You need to recheck your fit now and then, because your nipples may expand with breastfeeding and pumping (Meier, Motykowski, & Zuleger, 2004). In other words, you may see space around your nipples now, but this space may eventually disappear. If your nipples begin to rub along your pump's nipple tunnel, don't be surprised. This just means it's time to switch to a larger size.

5

Pumping and Milk Expression

For many mothers, pumping is key to reaching their long-term breastfeeding goals. In spite of this higher purpose, pumping is not fun. In fact, it is the part of lactation many women hate most. One of the top four reasons mothers give for weaning earlier than planned is the time and work of pumping (Odom, Li, Scanlon, Perrine, & Grummer-Strawn, 2013). This chapter will give you tips to minimize the time you spend pumping and maximize your milk yields so that you have more time for those things that you do enjoy.

Realistic Pumping Expectations

Do you have specific ideas of how much milk you think you should be pumping? If so, you're not alone. Unrealistic pumping expectations are the source of angst among many new mothers. Knowing what to expect can help you eliminate this item from your worry list.

What is the source of this worry? Many mothers compare their milk yield with the amount their friend or neighbor pumps, or they compare the milk they pump now with the milk they pumped for a previous baby. Before you judge your own results, you first need to know how much pumped milk is average. Many discover—to their surprise—that when they compare their own milk yields with the norm, they're doing just fine. Take a deep breath and read on.

Expect Less Milk during the First Month

If the first month of breastfeeding is going well and you're exclusively breastfeeding, your milk production dramatically increases from about 1 oz. (30 mL) on Day 1 to a peak of about 30 oz. (900 mL) per baby around Day 40 (see Table 3-1 in Chapter 3). Draining your breasts well and often naturally boosts your milk during these early weeks. At first, while your milk production is ramping up, expect to pump less milk than you will later. If you pumped more milk for a previous child, you may be thinking back to a time when your milk production was already at its peak rather than during the early weeks while it was still building.

Practice Makes Perfect

What should you expect when you begin pumping? First know it takes time and practice to train your body to respond to your pump like it responds to your baby.

At first you will probably only pump small amounts of milk, which will gradually increase as time goes on. Don't assume (as many do) that what you pump is a gauge of your milk production. That is rarely true, especially the first few times you pump. (Also, if you take a long break from pumping and then come back to it.) It takes time to become skilled at pumping. Even with good milk production and a good-quality pump, some mothers find pumping tricky at first.

> *"At first you will probably only pump small amounts of milk, which will gradually increase as time goes on."*

How Many Minutes to Pump

Have you heard conflicting advice about how long to pump? This may not be a critical issue while you are practicing with your pump before going back to work or if you have plenty of milk stored. In some situations, though, how long you pump can be key. Examples are if you're trying to boost your supply or you're back at work and pumping to keep your milk supply stable. When deciding how many minutes to pump, remember that "drained breasts make milk faster" and "full breasts make milk slower."

Science recently shed new light on this issue. During pumping, researchers measured milk-flow rates among 34 women (Prime, Kent, Hepworth, Trengove, & Hartmann, 2012). They found great differences from mother to mother. Some pumped 60% of their available milk within the first minute and were done quickly, while others pumped as much as 20% of their milk 14 minutes into their session. The most helpful discovery was that although the women's experiences varied, each woman's milk-flow rates during pumping were consistent during different sessions. In other words, women who pumped their milk quickly did so at every pumping, as did women whose milk kept flowing for longer periods.

What does this tell us? Simply put, that it doesn't make sense to give all women a one-size-fits-all set of pumping guidelines based on averages. Rather, you can determine your own best pump time by watching what happens during two or three pump sessions. If you find you're still getting a fair amount of milk after 15 to 20 minutes, you should pump at least this long. But if you get nearly all of your milk within 5 minutes, you can stop after six or seven minutes. Let your milk flow be your guide. Keep in mind, though, that these study mothers used the breast pump alone to remove milk. Before settling on a routine, try the hands-on pumping technique described later.

Factors That Affect Milk Yield

After you've made sure you've got a good pump fit (see previous chapter), you've had some practice with your pump, and it's working well, the following factors may affect your milk yield:

- Your baby's age

- Whether or not you're exclusively breastfeeding

- Time elapsed since last breastfeeding or pumping

- Time of day

- Your emotional state

- Your breast storage capacity

- Your pump quality

- Your pump suction setting

- Whether or not you use your hands

- Number of milk releases

Here is what you need to know about each of these factors.

Your Baby's Age

How much milk a baby consumes per feeding varies by age and—until 1 month or so—by weight. Because newborns' stomachs are so small, during the first week most full-term babies take no more than 1 to 1.5 oz. (30 to 45 mL) at feedings. After about 4 to 5 weeks, babies reach their peak feeding volume of about 3 to 4 ounces (90 to 120 mL) and peak daily milk intake of about 25 to 30 ounces per day (750 to 900 mL).

Until your baby starts eating solid foods at around 6 months, her feeding volume and daily milk intake will not vary by much. Although babies gets bigger and heavier between 1 and 6 months, their rate of growth slows down during that time, so the amount of milk they need per day stays about the same. (As explained in Chapter 7, this is not true for formula-fed babies, who consume much more as they grow.) When your baby starts eating solid foods, her need for milk will gradually decrease as solids take your milk's place in her diet.

Exclusively Breastfeeding?

An exclusively breastfeeding baby receives only mother's milk (no other liquids or solids) primarily at the breast and is gaining weight well. A mother giving formula regularly will express less milk than an exclusively breastfeeding mother, because her milk production will be lower. If you're giving formula, and your baby is between 1 and 6 months old, you can calculate how much milk you should expect to pump at a session by determining what percentage of your baby's total daily intake is at the breast. To do this, subtract from 30 oz. (900 mL) the amount of formula your baby receives each day. For example, if you're giving

15 oz. (450 mL) of formula each day, this is half of 30 oz. (900 mL), so you should expect to pump about half of what an exclusively breastfeeding mother would pump.

Time Since Last Milk Removal

On average, if you're exclusively breastfeeding, had some practice with your pump, and it's working well for you, expect to pump:

- About half a feeding if you're pumping between regular feedings. After 1 month, this would be about 1.5 to 2 oz. (45 to 60 mL).

- A full feeding if you're pumping for a missed feeding. After one month, this would be about 3 to 4 oz. (90 to 120 mL).

Time of Day

Most women pump more milk in the morning than later in the day. That's because milk production varies during the day. To get the milk they need, many babies respond to this by simply breastfeeding more often when milk production is slower, usually in the afternoon and evening. A good time to pump milk to store is usually 30 to 60 minutes after the first morning nursing. Most mothers will pump more milk then than at other times. If you're an exception to this rule of thumb, pump whenever you get the best results.

Your Emotional State

If you feel upset, stressed, or angry when you sit down to pump, this releases adrenaline into your bloodstream, which can prevent your milk from flowing. If you're feeling bad and don't pump as much milk as usual, take a break and pump later, when you're feeling more relaxed.

Your Breast Storage Capacity

As described in Chapter 3, this physical difference is determined by the volume of milk available in your breasts during their fullest time of the day. Storage capacity is based on the amount of room in your milk-making glands, not breast size. It varies among mothers, and in the same mother from baby to baby. Your largest pumping milk yield can provide a clue to whether your storage capacity is large, medium, or small (Mohrbacher, 2011). Mothers with a larger storage capacity usually pump more milk in a session than mothers with a smaller storage capacity.

If your baby is at least 1 month old, you're exclusively breastfeeding, and pumping for a missed breastfeeding, a milk yield (from both breasts) of much more than about 4 oz. (120 mL) may indicate a large storage capacity. On the other hand, if you never pump more than 3 oz. (90 mL), even when it has been many hours since your last milk removal, your storage capacity may be smaller.

What matters to your baby is not how much milk she gets at each feeding, but how much milk she receives over a 24-hour day. Breast storage capacity explains many of the differences in breastfeeding patterns and pump yields that are common among mothers.

Your Pump Quality

For most mothers, automatic double pumps that generate between 40 and 60 suction-and-release cycles per minute are most effective at expressing milk. This includes the rental pumps and professional-grade pumps described in Chapter 4.

Your Pump Suction Setting

Does common sense tell you that stronger suction will pump more milk? Not so. If your suction is set too high, discomfort (which can cause you to tense up) can actually prevent your milk from flowing. The best setting is the highest that's truly comfortable and no higher (Kent et al., 2008). This setting will vary among mothers, at different times, and could be anywhere on your pump's controls.

To find your highest comfortable setting, turn up your pump's suction until it feels slightly uncomfortable and then turn it down a little. Some mothers pump the most milk near the pump's minimum suction setting. A higher suction setting may be comfortable after your milk starts flowing, so try re-adjusting it upward then to see.

Whether or Not You Use Your Hands

Until recent years, we thought the breast pump should do all of the milk-removal work. Then a study found that mothers got 48% more milk when they used their hands while pumping (Morton et al., 2009). How does this technique, known as "hands-on pumping," work? Follow these steps:

"...a study found that mothers got 48% more milk when they used their hands while pumping"

1. First, massage both breasts.

2. Double-pump (pump both breasts at the same time), compressing your breasts often while pumping. Continue until milk flow slows to a trickle.

3. Stop pumping and massage your breasts again, concentrating on areas that feel full.

4. Finish by either hand-expressing your milk into the pump's nipple tunnel or by single-pumping, whichever yields the most milk. Either way, during this step, do intensive breast compression on each breast, moving back and forth from breast to breast several times until you've drained both breasts as fully as possible.

For the mothers in the study, this pumping routine took on average about 25 minutes total. For an online demonstration video, see "How to Use Your Hands When You

Pump" at this website: *newborns.stanford.edu/Breastfeeding/ MaxProduction.html.* Another plus of using the hands-on pumping technique is that it drains your breasts more fully, maintaining milk supply better and doubling milk-fat content (Morton et al., 2012).

Number of Milk Releases

As mentioned, stronger suction does not necessarily yield more milk. Why not? Because the key to effective milk expression is a muscle action known as let-down, milk ejection, or milk release. The number of milk releases you have during pumping can have a major effect on your milk yield.

Milk Release Is Key

What is a milk release? It is triggered by the hormone oxytocin, which causes the muscles inside the breast to squeeze your milk-making glands and push the milk out. Without it, most milk stays in your breast.

Some mothers feel milk release as a tingling sensation or see it as leaking milk, while others feel and see nothing. By watching your milk flow during pumping, you will see your milk releases as an obviously faster milk flow. During breastfeeding, you can hear milk releases when your baby begins gulping.

The fewer milk releases triggered during pumping, the less milk you'll pump. With no milk release, you'll express only the small amount of milk pooled around your nipples, which is at most about half an ounce (15 mL) per breast. This is one reason pumping isn't an accurate gauge of your milk production.

Without even realizing it, most mothers average about five milk releases at each breastfeeding (Prime et al., 2012). Some feel the first milk release, but very few feel those that come later (Geddes, 2009). Some mothers feel none. Even if you don't feel a milk release, your baby's swallowing and weight gain tell you they're happening.

While your baby is at the breast, milk release is triggered by her suckling, the feel of her soft skin against yours, her warmth, and your loving thoughts. Even when your baby is not breastfeeding, a milk release can happen when your breasts are touched, you hear your baby (or another baby!) cry, even when you think about your baby. Feelings of tension, anger, or frustration can block it.

When you pump, your baby's softness and warmth are missing. Suction from a piece of plastic feels very different from your baby's warm mouth and tongue. As you train your body to respond to the feel of the pump, you may need extra help to trigger milk releases. You may also need extra help when you switch from one pump to another, because the new pump has a different feel than the old pump. Mothers who have a regular pumping routine often say that following this routine is part of conditioning their body to release milk. The next section provides some tips for triggering more milk releases during pumping, which may increase your milk yields.

If you need help releasing your milk to the pump, try the following suggestions.

Use Your Senses

You can experiment with your senses to help condition your body to release your milk to the feel of the pump.

- **Feelings:** Get comfortable. Pump in a private place where you can relax. Close your eyes and imagine your baby at your breast. Breathe deeply and imagine a tranquil setting.

- **Sight:** Look at your baby or your baby's photo. Play a video of her.

- **Hearing:** Play an audio or video recording of your baby cooing or crying. Call to check on your baby, or call someone you love to relax and distract you.

- **Smell:** Smell your baby's blanket or clothing while you pump.

- **Touch:** Gently massage your breasts or apply warm compresses.

- **Taste:** Sip a favorite warm drink to relax you.

As needed, use whichever of your senses work best. Within a short time, you can condition your body to respond to the feel of your pump. You can also use these strategies whenever you're feeling stressed.

Vary Your Pump Speed

Most babies suckle faster at first to trigger milk release and then use slower jaw movements while the milk is flowing to drain the breast faster. If your pump has a speed or cycle control, try this approach to mimic your baby's rhythm.

- Start pumping on the "fast" setting.

- When milk starts flowing, go to a "slow" setting.

- Return to "fast" after milk flow slows or stops.

- Repeat until you see at least three to five milk releases.

If you have a two-phase pump with a let-down button, be aware that these pumps are programmed to automatically switch from a fast to slow speed after two minutes. That's how long it takes on average for a milk release to occur. If your body takes more or less time to let-down your milk, you can customize the pump to work better for you. For example, if your milk release occurs before two minutes, ress this button to switch to a slower speed as soon as it happens. Then return to a faster speed when your milk release ends and milk flow slows. You can use the let-down button several times during the pumping to speed up the milk-removal process. Your baby would do this automatically, but you can mimic this pattern by adjusting your pump according to your milk flow.

Double-Pumping: One Handed or Hands Free

Women often wonder how they're supposed to adjust their pump controls while double pumping. Are three hands required? Thankfully, no. Figures 4-1 in Chapter 4 and 12-1 in Chapter 12 show one way of double-pumping one handed. This makes it possible for you to turn your pump on and off, adjust your pump's suction and speed controls, or do breast compression and massage.

There are also many hands-free double-pumping options. Some pumps are marketed as hands-free pumps. The most costly models include bands and fasteners that make this process more difficult than it needs to be. Almost any double-electric pump can easily be converted to a hands-free pump with the right accessories. You don't need to overspend on your breast pump to pump hands free. For the most up-to-date listing of retail pumping bras and bustiers (bands that fit over your bra with button holes to hold your pump parts in place), do an internet search for "hands-free pumping."

There are also creative, lower-cost options. Some women buy inexpensive stretchy sports bras and cut holes in them to insert the pump pieces. Here are two internet tutorials on homemade options that use elastic hair bands and rubber bands:

- *http://kellymom.com/bf/pumpingmoms/pumping/hands-free-pumping/*

- *http://www.workandpump.com/handsfree.htm (be sure to click on the photos)*

Forgot Your Pump or Parts?

Sooner or later, nearly every pumping mother leaves something at home that's key to pumping. Here are some ways to plan ahead or handle it on the spot.

Bottles

- Keep a package of milk storage bags with your things at work and attach them to your pump parts with rubber bands.

- Go to the closest grocery or drugstore and buy standard-sized bottles of any size. Wash with hot, soapy water and rinse well before using, or buy some steam sterilizer bags and sanitize it in your workplace microwave.

Pump Left Behind or Useless Due to Missing Parts

- Keep a good manual pump with your things at work in case of emergency.

- Go to the closest baby store and buy a good manual pump. Either wash it in hot, soapy water and rinse well before using, or buy some steam sterilizer bags and sanitize it in your workplace microwave.

- Hand express your milk (see Appendix B) into any clean, wide-mouthed container.

- If missing parts, see if they're available to buy at the closest baby store or hospital gift shop.

Freezer Packs

- Keep your milk in the work refrigerator.

- Use ice sealed in Ziploc bags until you get home.

- In the pain relief section of the drug-store, look for cold packs used for sports injuries that chill when a seal is broken.

- See Table 6-1 in Chapter 6 for safe storage times at different room-temperature ranges.

If you'll be spending lots of time pumping, it makes sense to make it as easy as possible.

What If Pumping Hurts?

"No pain, no gain" does not apply to pumping. Just like during breastfeeding, pain while pumping is a sign that some adjustment is needed. If pumping is painful, consider these possibilities.

If you'll be spending lots of time pumping, it makes sense to make it as easy as possible.

Pump Suction Set Too High

As mentioned before, the highest suction setting does not always pump the most milk. Set your pump at the highest suction level that feels comfortable during and after pumping...and no higher. For some, this might be the minimum pump setting. Don't push the envelope. If you're gritting your teeth, it's too high!

Pump Doesn't Fit

Many mothers pump comfortably with the standard diameter nipple tunnel that comes with their pump. But if pumping hurts even on low suction, you most likely need another size. To check your pump fit, see Chapter 4.

Breast or Nipple Health Issues

If your pain is not due to too-high suction, or too-small or too-large nipple tunnels, ask yourself these questions. Do you have (or have you had) nipple trauma? If you had nipple trauma in the past, could you have developed a bacterial infection of the nipple? Do you have an overgrowth of yeast (also known as thrush or candida)? Could you have mastitis (see Chapter 3)? Does your nipple turn white, red, or blue after pumping? If it does, see your lactation consultant or other health care provider to rule out the circulatory problem Raynaud's Phenomenon and other causes related to breast and nipple health. Pumping pain may be a sign of a condition that needs to be treated.

The Feel of Hard Plastic

Some women find the feel of hard plastic on their breasts uncomfortable. If none of the above tips help, try using a soft pumping insert or a different style nipple-tunnel piece (one that some mothers find more comfortable is the Pump-in' Pal at *www.pumpinpal.com*).

Both Avent and Playtex pumps come with a soft silicone insert. Or you can buy soft inserts separately and try them with your pump. Options include the Avent Isis Petal Massager and the Ameda Flexishield Areola Stimulator. The Ameda Flexishield Areola Stimulator narrows your nipple tunnel to its smallest size of 21 mm, so this won't be a good choice unless you have very small nipples.

Less-Than-Average Milk Yield

Breast pumps work well for the vast majority of women, but there are exceptions. If your baby is gaining well and you are breastfeeding exclusively, you know your milk production is not the problem. (If you have milk-supply issues, see Chapter 12.) But if you've tried hands-on pumping and all of the other suggestions for improving milk yield in this chapter and you're still unable to pump even average milk volumes, it's time to try a different approach.

One option is to switch from a purchase pump to a rental pump. Some mothers get much better results with the types of pumps used in hospitals. To find one, visit the websites of Ameda, Hygeia, and Medela, which feature locators for local pump rental stations.

Another alternative is a time-tested approach used all over the world: hand expression. For some women, the skin-to-skin contact of hand expression greatly improves milk yield. In some cases, the pumping problem is due to unusual breast anatomy. The pump parts don't come in contact with the areas needed to effectively pump milk. Hand expression is a learned skill, but with practice, many women learn to do it quickly and efficiently. See Appendix B for instructions and links to video demonstrations of hand expression. See also Chapter 12, which includes tips for boosting milk production.

Now let's move on to how to store and handle the milk you express.

6

Milk Storage and Handling

Most mothers—whether employed or not—have questions about how to store and handle their milk. This chapter covers most of the basics, as well as some not-so-basic situations. It includes storage and handling options when traveling without your baby, which is part of some jobs. It also explains why some women's frozen milk develops a soapy taste (or worse), what you need to know about this, and how to prevent it.

What Your Milk Looks Like

You may be concerned the first time you notice your expressed milk looks very different from the cow's milk in the dairy case. Knowing why it looks different, and what to expect, may help set your mind at ease.

Layers

Over time, your pumped milk naturally separates into layers of milk and cream. Commercially sold cow's milk is homogenized, a process that prevents this separation from happening. Because your milk is not homogenized, expect that as it sits, layers will form. If these layers are obvious, before feeding your milk to your baby, gently swirl your milk, so that the cream mixes with the milk. This prevents the cream (which contains most of the milk fat) from being left on the sides of your container.

Colors

Expect color variations in your milk as time passes and with changes in your diet. During the first two to three weeks after birth, your milk is likely to be yellower than it will be later. In the last half of pregnancy and the first few days after birth, your breasts make colostrum (the concentrated first milk), which is often yellow or gold, but sometimes looks clear. As your milk increases in volume on the third or fourth day, it becomes transitional milk, a mixture of mature milk and colostrum. Finally, after the first two or three weeks, your milk is considered mature. At this stage, mature milk may appear bluish, yellowish, or even brownish in color.

Many women wonder if it is all right to feed their baby with milk pumped at a different stage of lactation. This concern is easy to answer. As long as you follow the milk-storage guidelines in Table 6-1, your milk will always be a good choice, even if you give early milk to an older child.

Some foods, food dyes, and medications can change the color of your milk (Lawrence & Lawrence, 2011). If you eat or drink something containing orange food coloring, for example, such as orange soda or gelatin, your milk may look a little pink or pink-orange. If you eat a large amount of kelp, or guzzle many green drinks, your milk may have a greenish tinge. If you've taken the antibiotic minocycline, your milk may even look black. Frozen milk may take on a yellowish hue, but it is not spoiled unless it smells or tastes sour.

It is not uncommon for your milk to have a reddish tinge during the early weeks. One study found that 15% of new mothers had red blood cells in their milk (Kline & Lash, 1964). Sometimes called "rusty-pipe syndrome," blood in the milk may be due to the extra blood flow to the breast, and the fast increase in milk production after birth. It is not a cause for concern and should disappear within a few weeks (Mohrbacher, 2010). Blood and milk have many of the same ingredients, and it is not only safe for your baby to drink this milk, it is head-and-shoulders better for your baby than nonhuman milks.

Milk-Storage Strategies and Guidelines

There's a lot to know about storing and handling your milk. This section covers best practices and explains why some milk-storage strategies are better than others.

Storage Strategies

When you're ready to start expressing your milk, review these recommended storage strategies.

How Much Milk Per Container?

Ideally, you want to store milk in the smallest volume you think your baby might take. The closer you can get to your baby's actual intake, the less waste there will be. You can always add more milk to a container, but because your milk mixes with your baby's saliva during feedings, most recommend that any milk left after feedings be discarded. (For more, see the section "Milk Left After Feeding" later in this chapter.)

If you need to store milk for a baby younger than 1 month, see Table 3-1 in Chapter 3 for average feeding volumes by age. For the baby older than about 1 month, a good starting point is to freeze 2-to 4-oz. (60 to 120 mL) of milk, which is about how much on average babies take from the breast per feeding (Kent et al., 2013). Smaller amounts thaw and warm faster than larger amounts, and you'll need to discard less milk if your baby doesn't take it all.

Once you're back at work, it will quickly become clear how much milk your baby takes from the bottle. Before you're sure about this, store some smaller, 1-to-2-oz. (30 to 60 mL) amounts, so your baby's caregiver can add a little extra if needed.

Fresh, Refrigerated, or Frozen

If your baby gets most of his milk directly from the breast, you don't need to worry about whether the relatively small amount of pumped milk he gets is fresh, refrigerated, or previously frozen. However, if a substantial percentage of your baby's daily milk intake is expressed milk, consider more carefully your milk-storage choices.

Freezing kills the live cells in the milk, which helps keep your baby healthy. So if a significant amount of your baby's daily milk intake is expressed milk, rather than freezing all of your pumped milk and using the oldest milk first, plan to feed your baby as much fresh or refrigerated milk as possible. This might mean keeping your freezer stash for emergencies and leaving what you pump each day at work for the next day's feedings.

Choosing Storage Containers

Does it matter what kind of milk-storage containers you use? In general, any food-grade container with a tight-fitting, solid lid (rather than one with a feeding nipple attached) can be used to store expressed milk.

There have been few studies done on container materials, and many of their conclusions are conflicting. This means that aside from stainless steel, which is not recommended because fewer live cells survive, there is no definitive best choice (Manohar, Williamson, & Koppikar, 1997; Williamson & Murti, 1996). One study found that more of one milk component (leukocytes) adhered to glass rather than plastic, which led to the recommendation that fresh milk be stored in plastic (Paxson & Cress, 1979). A second study found that different types of leukocytes react differently to glass (Pittard & Bill, 1981). A third study found that over time many of the leukocytes were released from the glass, and after 24 hours milk stored in glass had more leukocytes than the milk stored in plastic (Goldblum, Garza, Johnson, Harrist, & Nichols, 1981). Some recommend glass as a good first choice for freezing milk because it is the least porous, thus providing the best protection.

Avoid storing milk in polycarbonate plastic containers, which contain the chemical bisphenol-A (BPA). There are concerns that under certain conditions, this chemical could leach into the milk, and it is associated with possible health risks. As of this writing, however, polypropylene plastic is considered safe for milk storage.

Milk freezer bags have some practical advantages over hard-sized containers. They take up less storage space and can be attached directly to breast pump attachments in place of bottles. Because they are not reused, there is less to wash, but that makes them less eco-friendly. A 2013 study found that it's better to use glass containers rather than polyethylene milk bags for refrigerated milk because the bactericidal activity of the milk (which prevents spoiling) is better maintained in glass (Takci, Gulmez, Yigit, Dogan, & Hascelik, 2013).

Some types of milk bags are not recommended. Bags intended to be used as "bottle liners" are made mainly for feeding rather than milk storage, and tend to be thinner and more prone to splitting. If you use this type of bag, to safeguard your milk, insert your bag of milk inside another bag (double-bag it) before sealing and storing. Plastic sandwich bags are not recommended because they are thin and tear easily.

Because there is no one overwhelmingly best choice when it comes to milk-storage containers, feel free to use whichever option is most practical for you.

Why Milk Storage Guidelines Differ

It can be really unsettling to read different milk-storage guidelines in different places. Why do guidelines differ, and why can't the experts agree amongst themselves? There's actually a simple explanation.

Take a look at the milk-storage times in Table 6-1. Some are listed as "Okay" while others are labeled "Ideal." Within the "Okay" time ranges, pumped milk should not go bad. Over time, however, even though the milk is not spoiled, more vitamins, antioxidants, and immunological factors are lost. The shorter storage times labeled "Ideal" are the guidelines some organizations recommend because fewer of these milk components are lost.

The takeaway message is that while it is always better to use your milk sooner rather than later, your milk should not spoil if you store it within the "Okay" time frames. Stored milk that you find in the back of the fridge that has been there for up to eight days will still be far better for your baby than formula.

Some milk-storage guidelines also vary because they define "room temperature" differently. If you live in a subtropical climate, for example, the higher room-temperature range in Table 6-1 may be closer to your experience. But if you live in a more temperate clime, the lower range may be closer to yours.

You may have noticed that refrigerator storage times for fresh and refrigerated milk are longer than those for previously frozen milk. They differ because freezing kills the live cells in the milk, making the milk more susceptible to spoilage.

When in doubt about the freshness of your milk, smell or taste it. Spoiled milk will smell spoiled.

Table 6-1. *Milk Storage Guidelines for Healthy, Full-Term Babies at Home*

Tempurature	Deep Freezer (0°F/-18°C)	Refrigerator Freezer (variable) (0°F/ -18°C)	Refrigerator (39°F/4°C)	Insulated Cooler with Ice Packs (59°F/15°C)	Room Temperature (66°F-72°F/ 19°C-22°C)	(73°F-77°F/ 23°C-25°C)
Fresh	Ideal: 6 mos. Okay: 12 mos.	3-4 mos.	Ideal: 72 hrs. Okay: 8 days	24 hrs.	6-10 hrs.	4 hrs.
Frozen Thawed in Fridge	Do not refreeze	Do not refreeze	24 hrs.	Do not Store	4 hrs.	4hrs.
Thawed, Warmed, Not Fed	Do not refreeze	Do not refreeze	4 hrs.	Do not Store	Until feeding ends	Until feeding ends
Warmed, Fed	Discard	Discard	Discard	Discard	Until Feeding ends	Until feeding ends

Storage Guidelines for Full-term Healthy Babies at Home

The guidelines in Table 6-1 are specifically for full-term, healthy babies at home. If your baby is hospitalized, the time frames your hospital gives you are likely to be shorter. Preterm and ill babies are at greater risk for serious health problems, so your hospital may recommend you use stricter hygiene, such as storing your milk in sterile containers, or boiling your pump parts regularly.

These guidelines offer more options than many mothers realize. For example, you can refrigerate room-temperature milk at any point before its time is up. Depending on your room temperature, this would be before four hours (66°F to 72°F or 19°C to 22°C) or before six to 10 hours (73°F to 77°F or 23°C to 25°C). You can freeze refrigerated milk any time before eight days.

Power Failures and Freezer Stashes

Power failures are not uncommon. If you have a large freezer stash of expressed milk, you may worry about what will happen if a major storm or a power-grid failure cuts off power to your freezer for an extended time. If you find yourself in that situation, and you think the power failure will be short term, keep the freezer door closed to keep temperatures low for as long as possible. If your milk stays frozen, there's no issue. If it's possible to move your milk to a working freezer, consider doing so.

As you can see from Table 6-1, current guidelines recommend not refreezing thawed milk. Ideally, if your milk thaws, you will use that milk within 24 hours. But what if that's not possible? Do you really need to discard your milk?

Before tossing your milk, you should know the results of a study that examined the effects of refreezing donor milk expressed with normal hygiene (Rechtman, Lee, & Berg, 2006). The frozen milk was thawed at refrigerator temperature (39°F / 4°C) overnight, separated into different sample batches, and refrozen to -80°C (-110°F). These sample batches were later thawed to room temperature (73°F / 23°C), and each batch exposed to one of the following conditions: 46°F (8°C) for 8 or 24 hours, 73°F (23°C) for 4 or 8 hours, multiple freeze-thaw cycles of varying lengths, and the control batch kept at a steady -4°F (-20°C).

Bottom line, none of the batches developed unacceptable bacterial counts, and vitamin content remained at adequate levels. After this research was published, official milk-storage guidelines were not changed. In the case of a power failure, as you weigh your options, this information may provide some helpful perspective.

Safely Handling Your Milk

When you go to the trouble of pumping your milk, you want to make sure it stays as safe and nutritious as possible. The recommendations in this section will help you meet this goal.

Combining Batches

One of the most commonly asked questions about milk handling is whether you can combine the milk from one pumping session with another. Some mothers even ask whether it's okay when double-pumping (pumping both breasts at once) to combine the milk from the two containers afterwards. The answer to both questions is "yes."

If you add milk from your current pumping session to the milk from previous sessions, just make sure to date the milk according to the oldest batch. For example, if you add milk expressed on May 11 to refrigerated milk from May 10, the combined batch should be dated May 10.

Fresh milk can be added directly to refrigerated milk without cooling it first. Fresh milk can also be added to frozen milk, as long as there is less fresh milk than frozen milk, and it is first cooled for about an hour so that it does not thaw the top layer.

Thawing Frozen Milk

The best way to thaw frozen milk is by warming it gently and gradually, keeping heat low. Then swirl the milk to mix layers rather than shaking it. Freezing and heating your milk destroys some of its immune properties that kill bacteria, making it more vulnerable to contamination.

Milk can be thawed in the refrigerator overnight. Once thawed, it will be good in the fridge for up to 24 hours. You can also thaw or warm milk in other ways.

- Hold the container under cool running water for a few minutes.

- Hold the container in water previously heated on the stove. If the water cools and the milk is not yet thawed, remove the container of milk and reheat the water. Do not heat the milk on the stove burner directly.

If you use water to thaw or warm milk, tilt or hold the container, so the water cannot seep under the lid. Plan to feed thawed milk right away or refrigerate it (Jones & Tully, 2011).

Warming Milk for Feeding

When your baby is a newborn, it is best to warm your expressed milk to between room and body temperature before feeding. Older babies may drink chilled milk directly from the refrigerator. But for a small baby, cold milk can lower body temperature. Use either warm, running water or water warmed on the stove to gently heat milk for feeding.

Microwaves Are a No-No

A microwave should not be used to thaw or warm your milk. Why? Because it changes your milk's components and destroys much of its anti-infective factors (Quan et al., 1992). Microwaves also heat liquids unevenly, so even if afterwards the milk is swirled (or even shaken), hot spots remain that can burn your baby's throat.

Milk Left After Feeding

Most guidelines recommend discarding any milk left after a feeding because the milk mixes with the baby's saliva. La Leche League International is the exception: its milk-storage handout says that leftover milk can be used, but only at the next feeding (LLLI, 2008).

No published studies have scientifically examined the safety of feeding leftover milk, but a college student researched this scenario for her unpublished senior thesis (Brusseau, 1998). In her study, she divided fresh milk donated from six women into two bottles, one of which was warmed and partially fed to their babies. The leftover milk and the milk in the bottle not fed (the control milk) were cultured right after feeding and again 12, 24, 36, and 48 hours later. The only milk with higher bacterial counts was one batch of the warmed and fed milk from a mother who had not followed instructions, and had donated previously frozen instead of fresh milk. All other batches of milk showed no change in total bacterial counts within 48 hours after feeding.

This is an issue that affects many families, and there is little science behind the current recommendations. Hopefully, this information will help you make up your own mind about how best to handle your leftover milk.

Your Milk Is Not a Biohazard

It bears mentioning that one type of push-back related to milk storage and handling that employed mothers in the past have dealt with (and that we've hopefully moved beyond) is the fear that because mother's milk is a body fluid, it should be treated as a biohazard. American agencies and organizations, such as the Occupational Safety and Health Administration, the American Academy of Pediatrics, and the Centers for Disease Control and Prevention have issued statements confirming that human milk is not a biohazardous substance, and no gloves or other special precautions are needed when handling it: *http://www.cdc.gov/breastfeeding/disease/hiv.htm.* At workplaces and childcare facilities, your milk can be stored with other foods in a common refrigerator with no special precautions needed.

Options When Traveling Without Your Baby

In Chapter 2, Jessica E. from Illinois, USA shared her story about bringing her husband and baby with her during

her once-a-month work travel. Some mothers have the option of bringing their babies along, and some don't. If you'll
be traveling without your baby, either for work or for personal reasons, see Chapter 2 for recommendations on how
often to pump. Regarding what to do with your pumped
milk while you're traveling, you have several choices.

Figure 6-1. *It can be stressful to travel without your breastfeeding baby.*

Pump and Dump

Pouring your expressed milk down the drain is painful
for sure, even if you have a lot of extra milk at home. If
you have access to a refrigerator at your destination, keep in
mind that your milk will be good there for up to eight days.

While traveling, if you won't have easy access to a freezer to chill your pump case's cooling elements at night, bring many Ziploc bags with you to fill with ice and keep your milk cool. When it's time to travel home, you can also seal your milk containers in these bags to prevent leaking in transit.

Hand Carry Milk Home

When traveling home, you can hand-carry at least some of your milk home in your pump's cooling compartment and/or another cooler carrier. Your milk is good for at least 10 hours this way, and when you get it home you can then either refrigerate or freeze it.

In the U.S., see current Transportation Security Administration regulations on traveling by air with mother's milk at: *http://www.tsa.gov/traveling-formula-breast-milk-and-juice*. Here is a January 2014 excerpt from their website:

When carrying breast milk through security checkpoints, it is treated in the same manner as liquid medication. Parents flying with, and without, their child(ren) are permitted to bring breast milk in quantities greater than three ounces as long as it is presented for inspection at the security checkpoint.

When traveling by air, it may be helpful to bring a printed copy of the current guidelines to share with airport security if needed.

Ship Milk Home

A third option is to freeze your milk while you're away and ship it home. Obviously, access to a freezer at your destination is a must. If you are traveling for work, some companies will cover these shipping costs, which are not small. For recommendations on how to safely ship frozen milk from point A to point B, see: *http://newborns.stanford. edu/Breastfeeding/ShipNStore.html*.

Stored Milk That Smells Soapy or Rancid

Before amassing a huge reserve of frozen milk, it's a good idea to freeze several batches of your milk, thaw them after about a week, and then smell them.

Soapy-Smelling Milk

Some mothers make milk that has higher-than-average levels of the enzyme lipase, which over time, breaks down fat in expressed milk. This fat breakdown can cause cooled or frozen milk to develop a soapy smell and taste. Depending on the level of lipase in your milk, this change in smell and/or taste may occur sooner or later. Freezing slows but does not stop lipase from digesting the milk fat.

Safe for babies. This soapy-tasting milk is safe for babies, and many babies will drink this milk without a problem (Lawrence & Lawrence, 2011). Megan B. from Illinois USA returned to work full-time as a sales operations manager for a travel gear company when her son was 3 months old. She didn't realize until later in lactation that her milk was high in lipase, because it didn't affect her or her baby. "I didn't really know [my milk] was high lipase until just recently. My son drank the milk fine. It just had a soapy smell."

When it's a problem. This becomes a serious issue, though, if the baby will not accept the soapy-tasting milk. Marissa S. from Pennsylvania, USA describes an experience no mother wants to go through. "I remember crying when I had to throw away my freezer stash three days before returning to work. I was definitely not prepared for it!"

What you can do about it. The purpose of freezing a few batches for a week or more, and testing them for this soapy smell or taste is to avoid the need to discard a huge reserve of frozen milk. (Read on for other alternatives.) If your milk develops this soapy smell or taste and your baby accepts it, no problem. But if your baby doesn't accept it, what's next? Once your milk-fat is broken down, this process cannot be reversed.

If you find out in advance that high lipase levels may be an issue for you (mothers report their milk's lipase levels can vary from baby to baby), one approach is to scald your milk before chilling or freezing it to deactivate the lipase and prevent this fat breakdown from occurring. Heating your milk is not routinely recommended, because it kills live cells in the milk. But if baby will not accept your pumped milk otherwise, this makes it possible for your milk to be used (Jones & Tully, 2011). How should you scald your milk?

- Heat your milk in a pan on the stove until small bubbles form around the edges, but it is not yet at a full boil.

- Cool it quickly.

Jenn G., a full-time special-education teacher from South Carolina, USA, found herself in this situation.

Soon after giving birth, I started pumping, as I was going back to work when my daughter was 18 weeks old. After 14 weeks of pumping and feeding on demand, I had nearly 300 oz. (9000 mL) of breast milk stored. It was around this time that I offered my daughter a frozen bottle of milk. She refused it. I offered a second bottle, and she refused that. I smelled the milk, and it had a very soapy smell to it. I, of course, looked that up right away on Google and read about lipase. I thawed three more bags of milk, they all had that smell, and she refused them. So here I was about four weeks before returning to work with no useable milk, even though I had nearly 275 oz. (8250 mL) in my freezer.

I quickly learned that I would need to scald my milk. I took 5 oz. (150 mL) of freshly pumped milk and put in into five one-ounce bottles. I checked each bottle every five hours to see when my milk started to taste and smell bad. I found out that it was around hour 26. So I knew I could get through my entire school day without having to scald it at school. As soon as I got home each day, I began what my family affectionately called my science-fair experiment. I would scald all my milk. Then I would quickly put it all in glass bottles and cool it.

Not every mother with high milk lipase levels scalds her milk. Serena C. from Montana, USA structured her day so that she could exclusively breastfeed without using frozen milk at all.

We found ways around, it including breastfeeding on my lunch break, and then sending home the earlier pumped milk for later, as well as some reverse cycling. I ended up donating my whole freezer stash to a milk bank.

If this extra work concerns you, it may help to know how others have either fit scalding their milk into their busy lives or found ways to reduce the need for it.

When Michelle R. from Wisconsin, USA, a full-time teacher, discovered that her milk was high in lipase and her freezer reserve had gone "bad," she did some online re-search and some experiments. She found that in her case, it took three days for the change in smell and taste to occur, and she felt overwhelmed at first. "Didn't I already have enough to deal with: working full-time, pumping, and then being a mama the rest of the time?" But she soldiered on and discovered that she only needed to scald her milk once a week.

Figure 6-2. *Some mothers with high lipase levels in their milk scald their milk. Others find ways to avoid it.*

I developed a system where I used that day's fresh milk for the next day's daycare supply. On Friday, I would collect the milk and scald it in a pot, place the pot on ice just until it cooled, and finally pour it into storage bags. Come Sunday night, I would place those bags in the fridge to prepare for Monday at daycare. I felt very fortunate that I only had to do this on Fridays.

The previous mothers who shared their stories either donated their soapy-smelling milk to a milk bank or discarded it. But if you discover your milk has developed a soapy smell, before getting rid of it, know that there may be ways to use it even after the fat breakdown has occurred.

Some mothers find that their baby will take soapy-smelling milk if it is mixed with fresh or refrigerated milk. If you decide to use some of this milk, what ratio of soapy milk to fresh milk will make it acceptable to your baby? This varies by lipase level and by the baby. To find your best ratio of soapy-smelling milk to refrigerated milk, start with a half-and-half mixture. If the baby accepts that, you may want to try two-thirds to one third. Keep experimenting until you find the most soapy-tasting milk per container your baby will accept. That will allow you to use your freezer stash rather than pouring it down the drain.

Some sensitive babies even refuse milk that has been scalded. Marissa S., a full-time behavior specialist from Pennsylvania, USA, was extremely stressed when she found out that three days before going back to work that her baby refused her stored milk. By adding it to fresh milk, she found a way around it.

> One thing I found out through trial and error was that if my pumped milk was fed within 24 hours, the fats did not break down too much and my daughter would still drink it. When I knew I would need to re-frigerate or freeze my milk for more than a day, that night I would scald it before bed, and make sure to label everything clearly so that I could use the oldest first. I found my picky daughter really didn't like the scalded milk much, so I would freeze them in one-ounce stick forms to add an ounce or two to fresh bottles as needed, which she tolerated much better. I was the only person who did the scalding, as it is such a delicate process, and I didn't want to put the stress on my husband. I knew I would've been upset if the milk was over-processed.

These mothers did the scalding themselves. But in some families, the mother's partner could take on this task.

Sour or Rancid-Smelling Milk

If you use the milk-storage guidelines in Table 6-1 to store your milk and it becomes sour or rancid-smelling within its time frames, this change is probably unrelated to spoilage or milk-lipase levels. According to some food-storage experts, the most likely cause is chemical oxidation (Jones & Tully, 2011). One way to know if chemical oxidation is the cause is to scald some batches of your freshly pumped milk before freezing or cooling it (see previous section). In this case, heating will speed this breakdown, making the smell worse instead of better.

If sour or rancid-smelling milk is an issue for you, you may be able to prevent this change by avoiding free copper or iron ions in your water and polyunsaturated fats in your diet. Here are some specific changes that may help.

- Avoid drinking your local tap water; switch to bottled water for a while.

- Stop taking any fish-oil or flaxseed supplements.

- Avoid any foods, like anchovies, that contain rancid fats.

- Avoid using local tap water while handling your milk and its containers.

- Increase your intake of antioxidants by taking beta-carotene and vitamin E supplements.

Now that we've covered the current recommendations for milk storage and handling, as well as some special situations, next up are the how-to's of feeding your baby with bottles and cups.

7

Breast and Bottle Primer

Do you wonder which brand and style of bottle is best? This chapter explains what we know about choosing a bottle and how your baby's response can help you recognize when you've found a winner. It also covers the basic differences between breast and bottle, so that you know what to expect. Keep in mind, though, that if you're going back to work when your baby is 7 months or older, one possibility is to skip bottles completely and instead transition to a cup, which is covered in the next chapter.

How Bottle and Breast Differ

One often-overlooked reason breastfeeding norms can be so baffling to so many is that most of us grew up watching babies bottle-feed. Why does this matter? Simply put, people's minds and hearts absorb cultural norms like sponges. They become a part of us, affecting what our gut tells us, and what feels "right." Bottle-feeding and breastfeeding norms differ, and when you breastfeed, it helps greatly to know how they differ so you can tell good advice from bad. Knowing the differences can also help you avoid incorrect assumptions so that your decisions move you towards your goals rather than away from them. Many mothers base their choices—consciously or unconsciously—on what they know about bottle-feeding and sometimes unwittingly undermine breastfeeding in the process.

Feel and Flow

"Feel," as used here, applies to two aspects of feeding: how the feel of a mother's body affects her baby's inborn feeding reflexes, and the feel (firmness or softness) of the nipple in the baby's mouth.

Nipple Feel

It's important to know that it doesn't really matter to your baby how far your nipple protrudes. If you have ever compared your nipple to a bottle nipple and felt inadequate, you're not alone. The good news is that babies aren't born expecting their mothers to have long, firm bottle nipples. In fact, a nipple isn't even required. Newborns latch onto all kinds of body parts, including necks, shoulders, and arms.

To trigger active suckling, though, babies need a big enough mouthful of breast (a deep latch) so that your nipple extends into the "comfort zone," as described in Chapter 3. To find the area in your baby's mouth that triggers

172

active suckling, let your baby draw in your finger, pad side up, until it reaches the place where she starts sucking quickly. You almost never hear about a formula-fed baby having trouble latching onto a firm bottle nipple because it can be pushed back to that trigger area, even during sleep.

The breast, on the other hand, is soft. This is why no bottle nipple—whether latex or silicone—can ever be truly "like mother's breast." Because it's soft, your breast can't (and shouldn't) be pushed into the back of baby's mouth like a firm bottle nipple. Thankfully, nature has programmed your baby to take an active role in latching onto your breast, making this latching dynamic very different from what we're used to seeing with bottle-feeding.

Touch and Feeding Reflexes

Just like every other mammal newborn, our babies are born with reflexes that help them get to the breast and feed. Some of these reflexes move your baby to the breast, some help the baby attach to the breast, and some help the baby get milk from the breast. The feeding positions we use can have a major effect on how easy or hard it is for the baby to latch. And as we discovered in recent years, natural breast-feeding positions are very different from the positions used to bottle-feed.

The main trigger for our babies' inborn feeding behaviors is the feel of the mother's body against the baby's entire front, including face, torso, hips, and feet. U.K. midwife and researcher Suzanne Colson identified these triggers and many of the inborn feeding reflexes (Colson, Meek, & Hawdon, 2008). She and her team concluded that, like kittens and puppies, our babies breastfeed best on their tummies with gravity helping. When mothers in her study leaned back until they were semi-reclined and their newborns were laid tummy down on their bodies (Figure 7-1), breastfeeding went much more smoothly (also see Chapter 3).

Figure 7-1. *Natural feeding positions like this one make early breastfeeding easier because gravity works in harmony with baby's inborn feeding reflexes.* ©2014 Family Health Coaching. Used with permission

On the other hand, when the study mothers sat upright or laid on their sides (the positions most of us use to bottle-feed), gravity pulled their babies away from their bodies causing gaps, which sometimes disoriented babies and caused feeding problems (Figure 7-2). In these bottle-feeding positions, the same inborn feeding behaviors that made breastfeeding work well in the more natural, semi-reclined feeding positions often worked against breastfeeding. Head-bobbing became head-butting, and the baby's arms and legs flailed rather than helping them move toward the breast. Trying to breastfeed in bottle-feeding positions is the cause of many early feeding struggles.

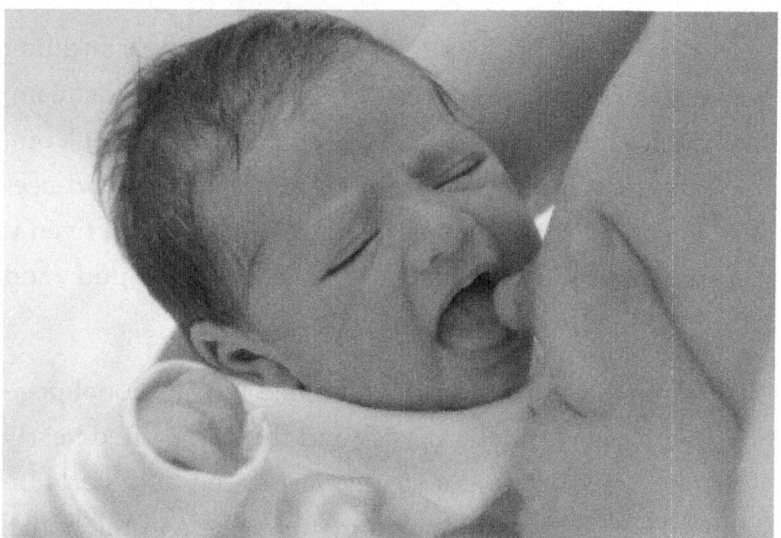

Figure 7-2. *When you sit upright to breastfeed, gravity pulls baby down and away, and baby's inborn feeding reflexes may actually make latching harder.*

Differences in Milk Flow

Milk flow from breast and bottle can vary greatly. And these differences in milk flow can have a major effect on how often and how long babies feed. At the breast, milk releases (aka, "let-downs" or "milk ejections") cause milk to ebb and flow. During milk release, your milk flows quickly.

Between milk releases, your milk flows slowly. On average, at the start of a breastfeeding it takes about a minute for fast milk flow to begin (Geddes, 2009). During an average breastfeeding, milk flow speeds up and slows down on average five times (Prime, Kent, Hepworth, Trengove, & Hartmann, 2012).

As explained in Chapter 5, when your baby's suckling causes the hormone oxytocin to enter your bloodstream, the muscles inside the breast squeeze, pushing the milk out. Some mothers feel the first milk release as a pins-and-needles sensation in their breasts. Others feel nothing. Even if you can't feel them, your baby's swallowing sounds and weight gain tell you they're happening.

In contrast, when babies bottle-feed in traditional positions, with your baby lying back and the bottle tilted nearly vertically, milk flows at a steady, fast speed and starts instantly. There's no waiting! No matter what's in the bottle, that consistent, fast flow means the baby has little or no control over when the feeding stops, increasing a baby's risk of overfeeding. For adults, too, eating quickly puts us at risk of overeating. That's why we are told to eat slowly so that our "appetite control mechanism" takes effect and we feel full with less food. One result of the natural ebb and flow of milk during breastfeeding is that babies' appetite control mechanism has a chance to take effect so they feel full with less milk.

Feeding Patterns

Both among newborns and older babies, scientists have found that feeding patterns vary greatly by breast or bottle.

Milk Intake Differences

Right from birth, research has found that bottle-fed babies take more milk per feeding and feed fewer times per day compared with breastfed babies (Sievers, Oldigs, Santer, & Schaub, 2002). One study measured milk intake at feedings in thousands of babies during their first 6 months and found that babies bottle-fed formula consumed much more milk at each feeding (49%, 57%, and 71% more at 1, 3, and 5 months respectively) than they did when they were breastfed (Kramer et al., 2004).

Formula-fed babies also take more milk over a 24-hour day. At 3 months, babies bottle-fed formula consumed 15% more milk per day than breastfed babies, and this increased to 23% at 6 months (Heinig, Nommsen, Peerson, Lonnerdal, & Dewey, 1993).

On a practical level, what this means to you is that you should not expect your breastfeeding baby to take nearly as much milk per feeding and over a 24-hour period as a formula-fed baby. If you have a neighbor whose baby takes a 7 or 8 oz. (210- 240 mL) bottle, don't expect your breast-fed baby to do the same. If your baby's caregiver has had more experience with formula-fed babies, you may need to explain this so that she can adjust her expectations. Larger feedings are normal for formula-fed babies, but not for breastfed babies.

Depending on how your baby is bottle-fed (see the next chapter), this may mean her feeding pattern will be very different while you're at work than when you're together. Don't be surprised if while fed by bottle, your baby takes more milk at feedings and feeds fewer times per day.

Realistic Expectations as Your Baby Grows

There are other feeding dynamics that are helpful to know. If bottle-feeding forms our expectations, we might believe (as many do) that during the first 6 months, as babies grow bigger and heavier, they will need more milk per day. We might also believe that during this time, they need fewer feedings per day. However, when it comes to the average breastfeeding baby, neither of these assumptions is true.

Between 1 and 6 months, the number of feedings and the volume of milk consumed per day by the average breastfed baby does not vary by much (Kent et al., 2013). Yet, there is often a big difference from one breastfed baby to the next in terms of how long and how often they breastfeed to get the milk they need. Between 1 and 6 months, the physical difference known as "breast storage capacity," which varies among women (see Chapter 3), has a much greater impact on feeding patterns than your baby's age.

As your baby gets older, mothers are often advised to try to stretch out the time between feedings. This may be valid advice when babies are bottle-fed, but not for breast-fed babies. Because breast storage capacity is a physical difference, trying to change a baby's feeding pattern by imposing a feeding schedule or doing sleep training can bring unintended results. If the mother has a small storage capacity, for example, going for longer stretches between feedings can cause her milk production to slow. In many families, when mothers try to use what they know about bottle-feeding to breastfeed, it leads to problems such as slow weight gain.

The Breast Is Never Empty

For many, this major difference between breast and bottle requires a huge change in mindset. A bottle can definitely be empty, but your breasts can't. Even if your breasts are well drained, because milk production is nonstop, there's always more milk available. While your baby is nursing from one breast, the other breast continues to make milk.

Because many mothers are more familiar with bottle-feeding, they assume that when their baby takes both breasts that they are now "empty." Sometimes they also assume there's no more milk from the way their breasts feel, which is not a reliable gauge. Lots of milk can be left in a soft breast. If the baby still seems hungry, they may assume formula is needed, which is usually not true. Rather than giving each breast more than once, which will provide more milk and boost milk production, they supplement, which if done often, can slow milk production.

As explained more fully in Chapter 3, on average, the first time a breastfed baby takes a breast, she takes about two thirds of the milk that's there. That means after taking both breasts once, usually one third of the milk is still available from each breast. If your baby still seems hungry, put her back to the first breast, where she will continue to get milk. You can give each breast as many times as your baby is willing. Breastfeeding researchers even have special names for how many times babies take a breast per feeding. Being done after one breast is an "unpaired" feeding, both breasts is a "paired" feeding, and taking each breast more than once is a "clustered" feeding (Kent et al., 2006). Rather than containers that are quickly drained, think of your breasts as always flowing fountains of milk.

Now that you have a clearer idea of some major ways breast and bottle differ, next on our agenda is what you need about choosing a bottle.

Choosing a Bottle and Nipple

In most baby stores, you'll see a vast array of bottles and nipples with claims on their packaging. Do some really reduce gas and colic? Is one nipple a better shape for a breastfeeding baby? Is one really "more like the breast"? How much of this marketing is hype? You'd be wise to assume all of it is hype. This section focuses on which product features are more likely to actually matter (and not matter) to you and your baby as you make your choices.

Bottle System or Interchangeable Parts?

To be frank, the bottle you choose is not likely to matter. What's more important is the nipple (also known as the teat), which is covered in the next section. However, you may appreciate knowing that feeding bottles come in two main sizes, standard and non-standard. The standard-size bottles and related parts are interchangeable among brands. You can use a nipple from one company, a collar from another, and a bottle from a third and they should fit well together without leaking. The non-standard type, though, is made in a unique size that only fits that brand. Examples of non-standard bottle systems are Dr. Brown's and Avent. You may want to think about this in advance and decide which path you want to go down. Once you start investing in the non-standard bottle systems, none of their parts will fit the other brands.

What about other bottle differences: slanted, vented, solid, or liner holders? The only one difference that may matter is the material that comes in contact with your milk, which was covered under "Choosing Storage Containers" in Chapter 6. Keep in mind that all the talk about bottle design preventing babies from swallowing air is baseless. Babies are meant to swallow air. It is impossible to stop, and it wouldn't be good for your baby if you could. Burping brings any air up, and gas is produced during the digestion of food, not from swallowed air.

Choosing a Nipple

Because babies are unique, the bottle that worked well for your neighbor's baby might not be a good choice for yours. This section covers some aspects to consider when choosing a nipple.

What to Look for in a Nipple

How do you choose among the many different nipple types and styles? Let's start with the basics.

Nipple length. Babies differ in many ways, including the shape of their mouths, which affects which nipple is easiest for them to handle. Texas lactation consultant Barbara Wilson-Clay did an experiment to learn more. She measured the mouths of 98 babies she saw in her lactation practice by letting them suck on her gloved finger until they drew it back to the area in their mouths where active sucking was triggered. She then marked with an ink pen the spot on her finger where their lips closed. This distance, which she called their "oral reach," ranged from 1.9 to 3.2 cm (Wilson-Clay & Hoover, 2013). This difference in mouth anatomy explains why some babies feed better with shorter or longer bottle nipples. You'll soon discover your baby's best fit by experimenting with different nipples. If your baby gags when she latches onto the base of the nipple, where her lips should close, that nipple is likely too long. If your baby's lips close on the bottle collar rather than the base.

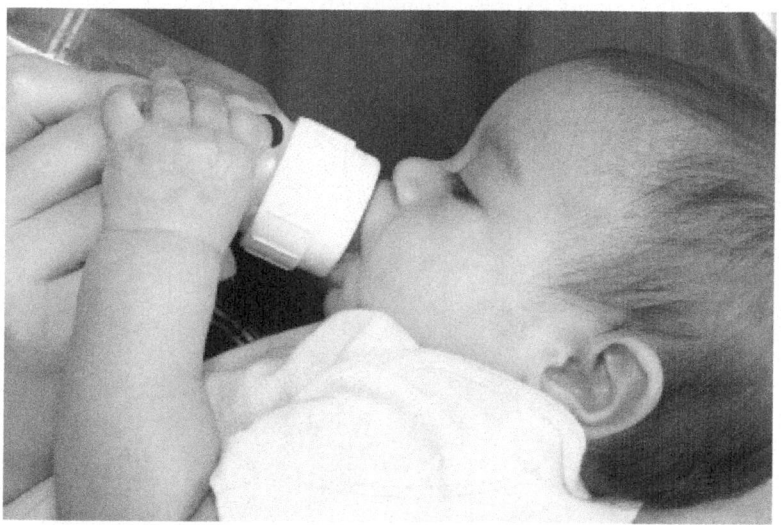

Figure 7-3. *This baby's lips are well flanged, but they rest on the bottle's collar rather than its base, so the nipple may be too short for her.*

Nipple shape. Although we have no hard evidence on which bottle nipple shape is best for breastfeeding babies, we do have some expert opinions. Lactation consultant Amy Peterson and speech-and-language pathologist Mindy Harmer compiled their personal and professional insights in the book, *Balancing Breast and Bottle*. In it, they suggest starting with nipples that widen gradually rather than those that widen abruptly, which in their experience are harder for many babies to manage (Peterson & Harmer, 2010). See

Figure 7-4 for an image that illustrates this nipple-shape difference.

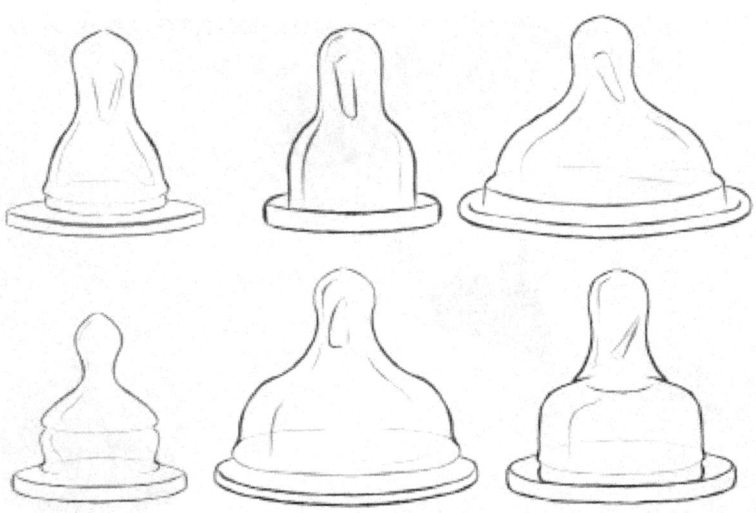

Figure 7-4. *Top row: gradual nipple widening. Bottom row: abrupt nipple widening.* ©2014 Anna Mohrbacher. Used with permission. Adapted from, *Balancing Breast and Bottle*, by Amy Peterson and Mindy Harmer.

In addition to how quickly or gradually a nipple widens, you may also come across different nipple types, such as the "orthodontic" (flattened on top) nipples, straight nipples, and those with a wide base. Each of these nipple types make claims about their benefits, but again, this is more a matter a preference. Let your baby decide which works best for her.

Nipple material. The vast majority of bottle nipples come in either silicone or latex. Silicone is firmer and more durable. Latex is softer, less durable, and can sometimes cause allergic reactions. Neither silicone nor latex feel like the breast to your baby. (Babies know bottle nipples are not the real thing from their smell and taste, as well as their feel.) Unless you or your baby has a latex allergy, one is not necessarily better than the other.

At this writing, there are some new nipples available that have a gradual transition shape but are so soft that they cause problems for some babies. A combination of a texture that is too soft and a gradual transition may cause baby's lips to slide to the nipple tip, rather than resting on the nipple base. A combination of a gradual shape and a firmer texture is ideal (Amy Peterson, personal communication, May 2014).

Nipple flow rate. For the breastfeeding baby, there are very good reasons to choose the slowest-flow nipple that works well for her. As explained earlier in this chapter, a faster milk flow increases risk of overfeeding. If a nipple has a really fast milk flow, your baby may take twice the milk that she actually needs while you're at work. By feeding your baby as slowly as possible, she will feel full with the least possible amount of expressed milk. This is good for both of you. You need to provide less pumped milk, and it establishes healthy eating habits in your baby.

Many bottle nipples have their flow rates printed on their packaging. However, this can be confusing because many seem to base their package recommendations on the baby's age. The slowest flow might be labeled "newborn" or "Stage 1." For the breastfeeding baby, though, flow is not at all about age. It's better to stay with the slowest flow possible for as long as your baby is bottle-fed rather than changing as she grows. This strategy keeps the amount of expressed milk you need to leave to a minimum.

Another clue to differences in flow rate is the number and type of holes in the nipple tip. Some brands' slow-flow nipples have one hole, and the number of holes increases with flow rate. Others use a slit for their fastest flow

One aspect of determining flow that can be frustrating is that flow rates are not standardized. In other words, one brand's slow-flow nipple may be comparable to another brand's fast-flow nipple. That's why trying different brands and styles can be helpful.

How to Find the Right Nipple

If you're wise, you'll not be swayed by the marketing hype and will instead focus on your baby's response to a bottle nipple. What does that mean? Let's start with what not to do. Don't invest a lot of money in one brand of bottle or nipple based on its questionable marketing claims. Don't rely on the experience of another mother and baby (whose mouth may be a different shape than your baby's). Instead, try one of maybe three different types of bottles and nipples (no need to go crazy and buy dozens), and see which your baby prefers. One easy way to do this is to begin with those you receive as shower gifts.

Try the suggestions in the next chapter on when and how to introduce the bottle. You have a found winner if:

- Your baby's lips close on the nipple's base.

- Your baby sucks and swallows rhythmically and stays active without gagging or choking.

- Feedings take between 15 and 30 minutes.

If your baby loses interest in feeding, starts biting the nipple, or seems frustrated, the flow may be too slow. If baby gulps quickly, looks worried, or pulls her tongue back to stop the flow, the flow may be too fast. If the flow is right for your baby during bottle-feeding, she will seem calm and happy, and will look you in the eye rather than looking away (Peterson & Harmer, 2010).

The next step is when and how to introduce the bottle and cup, which I'll describe in Chapter 8.

8

Feeding Your Baby with Bottles and Cups

Now that we've covered choosing a bottle, if you're like most mothers in Western countries, you have questions about bottle-feeding. At what age should a bottle be introduced? How often should it be given? Who should give it? For some of these questions, there are no definitive answers, but this chapter explains what we do know, and offers suggestions to consider. This chapter also shares strategies that can help you and your caregiver make bottle-feeding more like breastfeeding, so that you can do both in greater harmony. It also covers the introduction of cups, which if you're going back to work when your baby is 7 months or older, may allow you to skip bottles altogether.

When and How to Introduce a Bottle

If you ask friends, relatives, and even health care providers when to introduce a bottle and how often to give it, chances are you will get widely varied and passionate responses. You'll hear stories about babies whose parents waited too long, or didn't give the bottle often enough, and the hardships that occurred when these babies refused the bottle completely. The fact of the matter, though, is that there is very little hard evidence about this. In this way, too, every baby is different.

When to Introduce a Bottle

A story I heard many years ago helped me put the angst that surrounds this issue into perspective. I was helping a breastfeeding mother who was returning to work at the Federal Reserve Bank when her baby was about 6 weeks old. At the same time, she had a co-worker with a new baby about the same age who was also returning to work. The mother I helped did just fine, but the co-worker had challenges. This mother had formula-fed from birth, and when she returned to work at 6 weeks, her baby refused a bottle during his whole first week at daycare.

I was astounded by this story and knew that if she had been a breastfeeding mother, she would have blamed herself. She would have been certain her baby's behavior was all her fault because she had not given the bottle early or often enough, and she would vow to do things differently next time. Obviously, that was not this mother's problem, because her baby had only ever been bottle-fed.

What happened? My assumption was that during maternity leave, this mother and baby had developed a strong bond, and that the baby took one look at the strange caregiver and reacted negatively. It was as if he was thinking, "I don't bottle-feed with anyone but my mother." This story shows that there is much more going on around giving a bottle than most people think. It is not a simple dynamic, and relationships definitely play a role. After hearing this story, I began suggesting that mothers arrange for their babies to spend get-to-know-you time with their caregiver before their first day of work.

In truth, we don't really know the best age to introduce a bottle, although many have passionate opinions. The most common advice is to breastfeed exclusively for the first three to four weeks before introducing a bottle. This strategy gives your baby the practice needed to first master breastfeeding, reducing the chances that he may have a hard time going back to the breast.

Most babies take both breast and bottle just fine. Unfortunately, they aren't born with labels, so you have no way of knowing if your baby can do both early without a problem or if it makes sense to wait a little while. Because it can be gut-wrenching for everyone when a baby refuses the breast, if possible, I think it makes sense to wait the three to four weeks.

How to Introduce a Bottle

Do you really need tips on how to give a bottle? After all, didn't most of us grow up watching babies bottle-feed? Because it's been our cultural norm, we don't usually see ads for bottle-feeding classes. We just assume it's easy to figure out. But if your goal is to bottle-feed in a way that's in harmony with breastfeeding, read on.

Who Should Give the Bottle?

There are two schools of thought on this. One says it's best if the mother avoids giving bottles entirely so that the baby associates bottles with the caregiver and breast with the mother. Those who suggest this approach say it reduces the risk that the baby will grow to prefer the bottle over the breast.

A newer line of thinking says the opposite. Its proponents suggest that it's best for the mother to give the bottle because she knows her baby best and can better gauge the baby's reactions to it (Peterson & Harmer, 2010). An added benefit to this approach is that the mother is usually more available to do this.

How do you decide? Flip a coin, or go with the approach that makes most sense to you.

Strategies to Prevent Overfeeding

As explained in the previous chapter, one of the biggest risks associated with the bottle is overfeeding, which is a problem for several reasons. If the milk from the bottle flows really fast, your baby may take a lot more milk than he actually needs while you're at work. This puts pressure on you to provide more pumped milk. Because the volume of milk your baby needs every 24 hours stays relatively stable, overfeeding at work can also lead to less breastfeeding at home, which can throw off your milk production (see Chapter 11). Consistent overfeeding is also not good for babies, as it promotes unhealthy eating habits, which may increase the risk for overweight or obesity (Li, Magadia, Fein, & Grummer-Strawn, 2012).

The best approach is to try to bottle-feed slowly and mimic breastfeeding dynamics as much as possible. In most cases, each bottle-feeding should take between 15 and 30 minutes. A baby 1 month or older should be satisfied after an average of the 3 to 4 oz. (90-120 mL) he would normally take at the breast. If your baby is younger or is not average and takes more or less at a breastfeeding, aim for your baby's usual intake. If he typically finishes at the breast very quickly, it may make sense for bottle-feeding to take less than 15 to 30 minutes. If feedings are taking longer than 30 minutes or your baby loses interest while bottle-feeding, try a faster-flow nipple.

Keeping bottle-feeding as slow as practical is also the kind thing to do. Science has found more signs of stress among preemies during bottle-feeding than during breast-feeding (Meier, 1988; Meier & Anderson, 1987). A fast, consistent milk flow is harder to control. Imagine trying to drink from a fire hose. If faced with choking or chugging, most babies do their best to chug, but it's not always easy. Thankfully, the following strategies (aka, the "two Ps") can help you make bottle-feeding more manageable for your baby. These strategies would benefit any bottle-fed baby.

Positioning. As with breastfeeding, plan to feed on cue when your baby shows signs of hunger (rooting, hand-to-mouth) but is not yet fussing or upset. The first "P" to help prevent overfeeding is positioning and involves the position of the baby and the bottle. Rather than using the traditional bottle-feeding position, with your baby lying on his

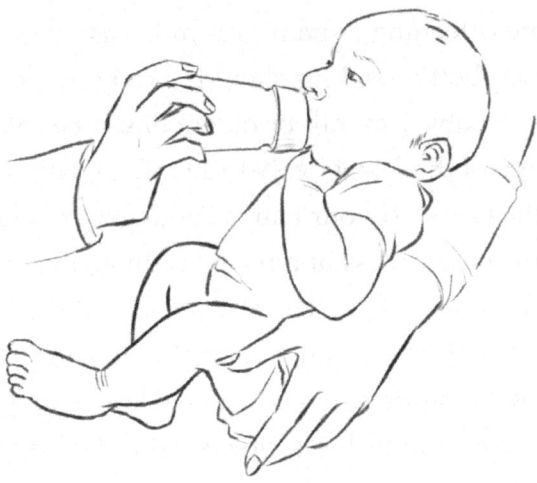

Figure 8-1. *Hold your baby more upright, with the bottle horizontal rather than vertical.* ©2014 Anna Mohrbacher. Used with permission.

Figure 8-2. *Touch your baby's lips with the nipple and wait until he opens wide before helping him latch on.*

back in your arms and the bottle held nearly vertical so that the milk flows fastest, hold your baby more upright and the bottle more horizontally, tipped up just enough so the nipple fills with milk (Figure 8-1).

With your baby held upright, begin by triggering a wide-open mouth. As with breastfeeding, ideally your baby will take an active role in latching onto the bottle.

- To trigger a wide-open mouth, try tapping your baby's upper lip with the bottle nipple or touching your baby's lips and chin with a gentle, sweeping up-and-down movement (Figure 8-2).

- When your baby's mouth is open, help him latch onto the nipple so your baby's lips close on the nipple's base rather than its shaft or tip. Latching deeply onto the nipple base will help prevent your baby from developing bad habits with the bottle that can cause breastfeeding problems.

- Check to make sure both your baby's top and bottom lips are flanged out. If they aren't, you can use your fingers to roll them out. If this continues to be an issue, you may want to try a different nipple shape.

If your baby gags when he latches onto the nipple base, this is a sign you either need to use a shorter nipple or the milk is flowing before your baby begins sucking and a slower-flow nipple may be better.

Pacing. The second "P"—pacing—lets you more closely mimic the ebb and flow of the milk during breastfeeding. This way of feeding gives the baby more control over his milk intake.

- When your baby starts feeding from the bottle, build in a pause every few minutes by lowering the end of the bottle so that milk runs out of the nipple. An alternative is to remove the nipple from his mouth, resting the nipple on his lower lip.

- When your baby seems ready to start sucking again, tilt the end of the bottle high enough so that milk partly fills the nipple again or trigger a wide-open mouth so your baby latches again.

- Repeat through the feeding until your baby is done.

Again, expect bottle-feedings to take on average 15 to 30 minutes, and for babies older than 1 month to feel full after about 3 to 4 oz. (90-120 mL). However, let the baby decide when he's done. Just like grownups, babies don't always eat the same amount. Letting your baby set the pace builds healthy eating habits that can last a lifetime.

For step-by-step specifics to share with anyone who feeds your baby, download the Appendix handout, "For the Caregiver of a Breastfed Baby" at: *http://issuu.com/nancymohrbacher/docs/caregiverbreastfedbabymohrbacher.*

Snacks versus Meals

How much milk to give when you introduce the bottle may sound like a small detail, but it isn't. The reason it looms large, especially during maternity leave, is because if your goal is to exclusively breastfeed, it has a huge impact on how much time each day you spend pumping. Remember, during maternity leave, your top priority is getting in sync with your baby. There will be lots of time for pumping and bottle-feeding later.

If you want your exclusively breastfeeding baby to get a bottle regularly (see next section), think in terms of "snacks" rather than "meals" (Peterson & Harmer, 2010). Specifically, this means giving very small amounts of milk by bottle each day—maybe an ounce (30 mL) each time—rather than a full feeding, and once bottle-feedings are going well, do it less often. This approach has several advantages:

1. It gives your baby practice and familiarity with the bottle (presumably your main goal).

2. It has a minimal impact on normal breastfeeding patterns during a time when frequent feedings are important to establishing your milk production.

3. It minimizes your time spent pumping.

If you're an average pumper (see Chapter 5), you will likely express the amount of milk you need by just pumping once every other day in the morning about 30 to 60 minutes after your first feeding. You may even need to pump less often than that.

Let's consider the alternative. If instead you give one full bottle-feeding as a substitute for a breastfeeding, for a baby older than 1 month, this would consist of 3 to 4 oz. or 90 to 120 mL of milk. Giving a full feeding could negatively affect your breastfeeding pattern because if your baby takes more from the bottle than from the breast, he may go unusually long before the next feeding. Also, from a practical standpoint, if you're an average pumper, this means you would probably need to pump twice a day to supply this volume of milk. And that doesn't leave any stored milk for other occasions or for your work freezer stash.

As mentioned, few women enjoy pumping. Giving a full bottle-feeding of expressed milk every day requires lots of pumping during maternity leave, which may mean that very quickly you're pumping as often as you will be once you're back at work. Not ideal.

How Often to Give the Bottle

In this area, too, we have no definitive answers, but experience tells us that every baby is different, and there isn't one approach that will work well for all. Keep in mind that there are no guarantees. Some babies fed a bottle each day for their first 3 months decide at that point that they're not going to bottle-feed anymore. Others, who've never had a bottle, take their first bottle at 3 months and never look back. Just like the story earlier in this chapter about the formula-feeding mother whose baby refused a bottle at daycare, giving a bottle regularly does not guarantee that your baby will continue to take one.

That said, you may decide you want to give a bottle regularly because knowing your baby is taking it well gives you peace of mind. If so, what many recommend is that once your baby is taking the bottle well for several days in a row, you can give it less often. Every other day or even every third day is usually often enough to prevent your baby from forgetting how to bottle-feed.

If Baby Resists the Bottle

Many mothers' worst fear is that their baby will refuse a bottle altogether. This is rare, with one study estimating it happens with about 4% of breastfed babies (Kearney & Cronenwett, 1991). This same study also found that about one quarter of babies require some patience and persistence before they take a bottle consistently and well. Don't be discouraged if it takes a little time.

If your baby seems to be resisting the bottle, the most important thing to avoid is allowing the bottle to become a battleground. Continuing to try to give your crying baby a bottle can cause him to develop a negative association with it. Rather than fighting about it, it's much better just to put the bottle down, act like it's no big deal, and try another time.

If your baby has already developed negative associations with the bottle and is upset every time he sees it, you'll need

to devote some time to improving his outlook. The key to convincing him that the bottle is really okay is to make all time with the bottle pleasant and positive. Let him play with the bottle on his own with no pressure to take milk. Act like it doesn't matter if he takes it or not. Hold the bottle close to you both while you're playing, smiling, and talking.

Figure 8-3. *Try holding a reluctant bottle-feeder with his back against your body.*

Here are some other tips if your baby resists the bottle.

- Try varying the temperature of the milk. Some babies accept a bottle more easily if the milk is a little warmer or cooler.

- Try offering it at different times of day. Evening is when babies are fussiest and least likely to accept anything new. Try in the morning, when everyone is rested and more cheerful. Pick a time between feedings when your baby is not full and not too hungry.

- Use different feeding positions. Rather than holding your baby in arms in a breastfeeding position, try holding him with his back against yours (Figure 8-3), or offer the bottle from behind while your baby sits in a car seat or bouncy chair.

Use movement. Some babies will take the bottle better when you're walking or rocking, or even bouncing gently on a yoga ball.

If your baby will take the bottle but just doesn't seem to know what to do with it, try teasing him a little by trying to pull it out. Some babies will respond by sucking it back in.

Nancy Holtzman, RN, IBCLC, CPN, suggests a strategy she calls "Intermittent Bottle by Mom," or IBBM. To do this:

1. Have an ounce (30 mL) or so of freshly expressed milk in a bottle by your feeding spot.

2. Start breastfeeding as usual.

3. After a couple of minutes of breastfeeding, remove the breast and offer the bottle. If your baby takes it, fine. If not, it's no big deal.

4. If your baby didn't take the milk, after another five minutes or so, try the bottle again.

#1 Tip for Bottle or Breast Refusal

If your baby balks at either breast or bottle, the most important thing is to avoid any fighting or unhappiness. Focus on building positive feelings about it.

If your baby resists the bottle, bring it out only when your baby is calm and happy, and let her play with it. Don't push it. See the IBBM strategy in this chapter.

If your baby begins resisting the breast, focus on creating happy times at the breast with your baby, cuddling, talking, and playing there. Let your baby take a nap with her head resting on the breast. Lean back, and lay your baby tummy down near the breast. Take baths together and build in other times of skin-to-skin contact. Try doing "dream feeds" at the breast, when your baby is in a light sleep (look for eyes moving under eyelids).

She suggests doing this at three feedings each day. If your baby doesn't take the milk, she suggests putting the bottle in the refrigerator between feedings, rewarming and reusing it until the end of the day, and discarding any remaining milk then.

Creativity sometimes helps, too. In desperation, one father of a 3-month-old breastfed baby began spooning out some partly defrosted milk and feeding it to his baby like ice cream. His previously unhappy baby, although unwilling to take the bottle, was delighted to eat this new breast-milk "slushie" (Walker, 2011).

Bottle-feeding is a skill that differs from breastfeeding and can take time and practice for some babies to master. Despite what some people say, when babies have trouble taking the bottle, this does not mean they're "being stubborn." And it doesn't make sense to add stress to an already stressful situation by trying to starve them into taking it.

Cup FAQ

It's possible to skip bottles entirely, but nearly every baby eventually learns to use a cup, which is a life-long skill. Many mothers have questions about timing and strategies for transitioning baby to a cup. The following are some frequently asked questions.

At what age can a baby be fed by cup?

Would you believe that babies can cup-feed from birth? In the West, feeding bottles are common. However, in some parts of the world, bottle-feeding is discouraged. If extra milk is needed, tiny babies sip or lap it from spoons or small, straight-sided cups. Why? In developing countries, water for washing and drinking is not always safe, making it hard to clean bottles and nipples well enough. As a result, mother's milk can become contaminated by the bacteria that grow in the cracks and crevices of a feeding bottle. Even preemies can feed from these straight-sided cups with just a little practice. Canadian pediatrician Jack Newman shows cup-feeding in action in the following free online video: *http://www.breastfeedinginc.ca/content.php?pagename=vid-cupfeed.*

What about cups with lids? Most older babies can manage these on their own at about 7 to 8 months of age. Keep in mind that it may take a couple weeks of practice before your baby takes much milk from the cup.

What do I need to know about cups for older babies?

There are two basic types of commercial cups with lids:

- Cups with built-in straws

- Sippy cups with spouts

In general, cups with straws (Figure 8-4) are a better long-term choice. Creating a seal on the straw with their lips, sucking on the straw, and then swallowing are appropriate skills for an older baby to master. But you don't need to buy a commercial straw cup. See the next answer for details on strategies for using an open drinking container and a separate straw. Drinking from a straw helps your baby transition more quickly to the types of glasses and cups he will need to use as he grows. Learning to drink from a regular cup and through a straw are skills that babies will use for their entire lives.

Figure 8-4. *Drinking through a straw is a skill that lasts a lifetime.*

In contrast, the mouth movements needed to remove milk from a sippy cup are similar to those used with the bottle. A sippy cup can provide a good short-term transition from bottles, but it is not a necessary step. If a sippy cup is used for years rather than as a short-term transition, one downside is that it teaches tongue thrusting, which can negatively affect your baby's oral development. If sweet liquids such as fruit juice are inside the sippy cup, they can bathe your baby's teeth, which can contribute to tooth decay. For this reason, if you use a sippy cup, consider limiting its contents to water only.

What are some tips for getting started with a cup?

When an older baby starts drinking from a cup, put plain water in it while he learns so that you don't have to worry about sticky surfaces or your pumped milk being wasted. Often babies start by turning the cup upside down to see how much spills out and splashing in it. Give your baby a chance to practice with a liquid that is not so precious to you or so likely to make clean-up a challenge.

When you transition your baby to an open cup, or an open cup with a separate straw, a good time to start is when you are sitting next to your baby at mealtimes. While your baby is learning, it may help to shorten the straw by cutting it, as shorter straws require less suction to draw up liquid.

Expect it to take a little time for your baby to go from taking drops from the cup to drinking more. Just like when choosing a bottle, it may help to get a couple of different types and styles of cups to see which your baby prefers.

What should baby drink from a cup?

For babies between 7 and 12 months, either your milk or water are good choices, as well as clear broths. For babies older than a year, you have more options. Cow's milk from the store is one, which is high in protein and calcium. The American Academy of Pediatrics has long recommended using whole cow's milk until age 2 years, and then switching to 2% milk. Other types of "milks" (more accurately, juices) from beans, grains, and nuts (soy, almond, rice, oat, hemp) are available, too. Soy milk is high in protein. The other "milks" made from plants and nuts are low in protein, but some are calcium fortified.

Plan to keep fruit juice consumption to a minimum. As a natural sugar water, it is missing all of the fruit's healthy fiber. In fact, from a nutritional point of view, fruit juice is not much better than soft drinks. The American Academy of Pediatrics recommends that older babies and toddlers drink no more than 4 oz. (120 mL) of fruit juice per day, as more than this has been linked to health issues (AAP, 2001).

Now that we've covered the basics of cup and bottle-feeding, let's focus on your transition back to work.

9

Transition to Work

Do you wonder when you should start preparing in earnest for your return to work? This chapter offers some guidance on when to begin freezing milk, how much milk to store, and how to calculate the milk your baby will need during your work day. Since your top priority while on leave is to enjoy this time with your baby, you also need to know how to keep pumping to a minimum without short-changing your back-to-work planning. This chapter also explores whether or not you will be pumping at work, and your options either way. It also provides practical tips on scheduling, pumping shortcuts, and even your work wardrobe.

Freezing Milk for Work

How can you balance your time with your baby with your need to prepare for work? Let's start with some pumping strategies.

Pumping During Maternity Leave

While on maternity leave, many mothers spend too much time pumping. How much is too much? Perhaps a better understanding of the basics will explain.

Time to Practice

If you'll be pumping at work, try to allow at least three to four weeks of practice with your pump before your first day back. It takes time to condition your body to release your milk to the pump like it does to your baby. And this conditioning will be much easier to do while you're at home, where you can nurse the baby if the pump does not drain you well. Review Chapter 5 for details on how much milk you should expect to pump, so that you'll recognize when your milk yield is in the right range and you're ready for the workplace.

When to Start Storing Milk

If you feel pressure to start pumping and storing right after birth, take a few deep breaths. There are drawbacks to pumping too early. One is the low return on investment. During the first month—when your milk production is ramping up (see Table 3-1 in Chapter 3)—you will pump much less milk than you will later. If you're exclusively breastfeeding, pump average amounts of milk, and are pumping between feedings, at one week, your milk yield from both breasts is likely to be around 0.75 oz. (22.5 mL).

By four weeks or so, an average pump session between feedings yields more like 1.5 to 2 oz. (45-60 mL), which gives you much more milk in the same amount of time. Unless you're starting back to work before six weeks, you may want to wait. You will get far more milk for your freezer stash if you wait until your baby is at least three to four weeks old to start pumping and storing.

Figure 9-1. *During maternity leave, don't let pumping get in the way of enjoying your baby.*

What if you're returning to work much later? If you'll be starting work before your baby is about 9 months old and you want to store milk for your work days, allow about one month to build a healthy freezer reserve. For more details, see the next section.

Variables to Consider

Your pumping plan at home will depend in part on the length of your maternity leave, whether or not you plan to exclusively breastfeed, your work schedule, and whether or not you'll be pumping at work (a later section covers this last option).

Not exclusively breastfeeding. If you don't plan to exclusively breastfeed after returning to work, you can pump or not pump at home as you choose. Your pumping decisions will depend on your baby's age and how much of your milk you want to have on hand after you're back at work (see next section). If your baby will be older than 12 months when you start work, this is not a burning issue, as most employed mothers have stopped pumping by then anyway. While you're at work, babies older than 1 year can drink other milks and liquids, although your baby would certainly benefit from continuing to receive your milk if you choose.

What if your baby is younger than 1 year and you plan to provide your milk exclusively? See where you fit among the following categories.

Full-time job, baby younger than 6 months, exclusively breastfeeding. If you plan to provide your milk only for your younger baby, keep in mind that, very likely, you will pump enough milk at work each day to provide what your baby needs for the following day. When you're at work and missing feedings, expect to pump twice the milk you pump at home between feedings.

How much frozen milk should you have stored when you go back to work? Some of this depends on your comfort level. Will you feel anxious if you start work with less than a whole freezer full of milk? Or would you be happy to start work with just enough milk to cover the first day?

A good middle ground is to plan to have enough frozen milk for your first day back and some extra to cover the unexpected. If you and your baby are average, this would be about 12 oz. (360 mL) for the first day plus another 10 feedings of 3 to 4 oz. (90 to 120 mL) each. But you get to decide what feels right to you. If you're average and you pump once in the morning every day during the month before you return to work, that's about how much milk you'll accumulate.

If you'll be returning to work before your baby is 6 weeks old, you may need to begin pumping earlier and more often. In this case, since you'll be away from your baby during the time she would be breastfeeding intensively to stimulate a full milk supply, more intensive pumping can help you get there sooner. Although your pump yields may be low, pumping after at least three to four feedings each day and evening should boost milk production. (You need your sleep at night to recover from childbirth.) And you can combine these small batches of milk and freeze them for later. See Table 3-1 in Chapter 3 for an idea by age of how much milk per feeding your baby needs during the newborn period. In this situation, make sure you're draining your breasts well with the baby or the pump at least 8 to 12 times per day until you reach full milk production, which is about 30 oz. (900 mL) per day.

Full-time job, baby older than 6 months, providing your milk only. As babies eat more solid foods, they need less milk. A baby in the 6-to-8-month age range will still need either mother's milk or formula for much of her intake during the work day. Some babies are slow to take solids. In this case, use as a starting point the volumes mentioned in the previous situation: 12 oz. (360 mL) for the first day of work plus another 10 or 15 feedings of 3 to 4 oz. (90 to 120 mL) each. Again, adjust according to your own comfort level.

> What's a good freezer stash goal? If you'll be working full-time, aim for 12 oz. (360 mL) for the first day of work plus as a reserve for the unexpected, another 10 or so feedings of 3 to 4 oz. (90 to 120 mL) each.

If your baby is 9 to 12 months old, again with the addition of more solid foods, she will need less milk. It's also normal for your milk production to decrease as your baby takes more other foods. So don't be surprised if your pumping volumes are lower than before. Because babies' intake of solid food varies so much, it is difficult to predict exactly how much milk your baby will need during this stage.

Part-time job, exclusively breastfeeding. When you work part time, there are many moving parts involved. Your choices will depend on the specifics. Working 10 hours per week is obviously much different than working 30 hours per week. The length of your work day is also important. Will you be working a few long days or many short days? See Appendix C for sample work schedules and plans. Also look at the previous section if you're working full time. Use that as a benchmark and adjust downward accordingly.

When and How Often to Pump at Home

If you're returning to work after 6 weeks, the good news is that you don't need to pump often to build a healthy freezer stash.

How often to pump. If your baby is older than 6 weeks and your goal is to store maybe 12 oz. (360 mL) for the first day back and 10 more feedings in your freezer, it only takes 1 daily pumping for a month to build a

"..it only takes 1 daily pumping for a month to build a healthy reserve of milk."

healthy reserve of milk. If you're pumping between feedings and you get the expected half a feeding per pump session, pumping once a day for 30 days equals 15 feedings. Again, if you'll be pumping at work, you will likely be able to pump enough milk there each day for the next day's feedings. Your reserve is there to cover the unexpected.

When to pump. While you're on leave, to avoid upsetting your baby or shortchanging her need for milk, try to allow at least an hour between pumping and breastfeeding. On average, babies only take about two-thirds of the milk that's in the breast, so there is usually milk left to express after a feeding (Kent, 2007). If you wait a little while before pumping, you'll get even more milk. Try these tips:

- Pump in the morning, as most women get more milk then than later in the day.

- Pump 30 to 60 minutes after a breastfeeding.

Another option is to pump one breast while your baby breastfeeds from the other breast. This works especially well if your baby usually takes one breast per feeding.

If your baby wants to breastfeed right after you pump, go ahead. Most babies are patient and don't mind feeding longer. Your baby can go back and forth from breast to breast several times if needed. Milk is constantly being produced, so even if you just finished pumping, there will be milk for your baby.

Your Baby's Milk Needs During the Work Day

To calculate your baby's milk needs during the work day, let's first focus on the bigger picture. Typically, milk production reaches its peak at about 5 weeks and stays re-markably stable until about 6 months (Kent et al., 2013). At 6 months, as your baby takes more solid foods, her need for milk decreases.

Your Baby's 24-Hour Milk Intake

On average, 1-to-6-month-old breastfed babies consume about 30 oz. (900 mL) of milk per 24-hour day. However, not every baby is average. Some breastfed babies gain weight well on much less milk; others on much more. One study measured 24-hour milk intake in 71 thriving exclusively breastfed babies and found their daily milk intake ranged from 16 oz. (480 mL) to 42 oz. (1220 mL). That's a huge range! Some took almost triple the milk of others. What this means to you is that you don't need to panic if the 30-oz. (900 mL) average does not seem right for your baby. What's most important is that your baby has a healthy weight gain, which is about 1 oz. (30 g) per day for the first three months and less as baby gets older.

That said, let's use the 30-oz. (900 mL) average as a benchmark for calculating your baby's need for milk during your work day. It will quickly become obvious if these num-bers are off, and you can adjust if needed. For example, most breastfed babies take on average 3 to 4 oz. (90 to 120 mL) of milk per feeding, which is a good place to start when choosing your batch size. But some babies take more and others take less. Sarah C., a holistic health practitioner from Illinois, USA, discovered to her surprise when she returned to work full-time at seven weeks, that her baby never took more than 2.5 oz. (75 mL) at a feeding. Until you're sure how much milk your baby wants, you may want to start with smaller volumes and store some 1 and 2 oz. (30 and 60 mL) batches to add as needed.

Calculating Your Baby's Milk Needs

When calculating how much milk your baby needs while you're at work, ask yourself these questions.

How many hours are you apart, including travel time? And how much of the 24-hour day is that? For example, if you're away from your baby for eight hours, that is one third of the 24-hour day. One third of 30 oz. (900 mL) is 10 oz. (300 mL). The points below list several time frames and the average milk volumes you should expect your baby to need.

- 6 hours apart (one quarter of a 24-hour day) one quarter of 30 oz.(900 mL) is 7.5 oz. (250 mL)

- 8 hours apart (one third of a 24-hour day) one third of 30 oz. (900 mL) is 10 oz. (300 mL)

- 12 hours apart (half of a 24-hour day) half of 30 oz. (900 mL) is 15 oz. (450 mL)

Again, keep in mind that your baby will need about the same amount of milk per day at 5 weeks as he will at 6 months. Unlike the baby who is formula-fed, breastfed babies do not need more and more milk as they grow bigger and heavier because as they grow, their rate of growth slows (Kent et al., 2013; Kent et al., 2006).

Does your baby breastfeed during the night? This is important to know, too. The calculations above are based on your baby breastfeeding around the clock. However, if you have an unusual baby who sleeps for stretches longer than 4 to 6 hours, you need to calculate differently. For example, if your baby sleeps eight hours straight at night, this means she needs to consume all 30 oz. (900 mL) of her daily milk intake within the 16 hours she's awake. That's a very different equation! Because eight hours is half of your baby's 16-hour feeding day, this means that for an eight-hour work day, your baby will need half of her daily intake, or 15 oz. (450 mL). If you're apart for 12 hours, this is three-quarters of her waking hours, and she'll need three-quarters of her milk intake, or slightly more than 22 oz. (660 mL). Big difference! See Chapter 11 for more about the role night feedings can play in meeting your long-term breastfeeding goals.

Pumping at Work: Will You or Won't You?

Pumping at home is one thing, but do you wonder if pumping at work makes sense for you? If so, you're not alone. Before deciding whether to pump at work, it's wise to consider the pros and cons. Here are some points to consider.

Work Pumping Advantages

If your baby is younger than 1 year, isn't available to breastfeed during work, and you work long days, there are benefits to pumping at work.

- It keeps you comfortable and prevents the embarrassment of leaking milk.

- It decreases your risk of painful breast problems, such as mastitis (see Chapter 3).

- It helps maintain your milk production.

- It avoids some or all of the cost and health issues associated with the use of infant formula.

Work Pumping Challenges

Of course, pumping at work is not all sweetness and light. There are also downsides.

- It takes time away from work, which may involve arriving early or staying late to make up for lost work time.

- It reduces time spent socializing during breaks and meals.

- It requires finding a comfortable, private, easily accessible place to pump.

- It may mean dealing with push-back from employers or coworkers.

When considering your options, keep in mind that like breastfeeding, pumping doesn't have to be all or nothing. Even if you can't or don't want to pump the ideal number of times per day, some pumping is always an option. See the section "Challenging Work Settings" in Chapter 2 for ideas on how to fit in pumping or breastfeeding if your job makes this difficult.

Pumping Is Temporary

Keep in mind, too, as the first chapter describes, nearly all mothers stop pumping at work by or around their baby's first birthday. How long you decide to pump at work, of course, depends on your unique situation, as well as your baby's age. If your baby is a year or older, pumping might not even be on your radar. If pumping is part of your experience, however, don't forget that the need to pump is temporary. Knowing this may make it feel more manageable to both you and your employer.

If You Won't Be Pumping at Work

Much of this book describes strategies for mothers who pump at work. But if you don't plan to pump, you need strategies, too. You may wonder, for example, if you must wean completely to avoid painful breast fullness and leaking milk at work. The answer is no. You have a number of other options, as well. This section gives you tips for maximizing breastfeeding during your maternity leave while safeguarding your comfort and sanity after you return to work. It even includes options other than weaning.

Weighing Feeding Options

You may be surprised to know that even if you're working full-time and won't be pumping at work, you still have several options. Some are dependent, though, on where you fall on the breast-storage-capacity spectrum.

The Impact of Breast Storage Capacity

Breast storage capacity is a physical attribute that varies greatly among mothers and was described in detail in Chapter 3. Simply put, storage capacity is determined by the amount of milk your breasts contain during their fullest time of the day. It is based not on breast size, but on how much room there is in your milk-making glands. This individual difference has a major implications for employed mothers.

What is its effect? If your capacity is very large, you may be able to go through an entire eight-hour work day without breastfeeding or pumping, yet not suffer any negative consequences. This is rare, but I worked with a mother who did this successfully for four months. She breastfed when she and her baby were together, and was able to pump enough milk before and after work to provide exclusive mother's milk feeds for her baby while she was gone.

Although this worked for her, if your storage capacity is medium or small, your experience would likely be very different. For most mothers, staying very full of milk for eight hours could bring on the breast pain and swelling known as mastitis (see Chapter 3). Over time, it would also reduce milk supply. (Full breasts make milk slower.) This same approach could produce vastly different outcomes in different women.

How do you know where you fall on the breast-storage-capacity spectrum? You can't know exactly, but there are some clues that can help guide you as you weigh your choices.

What's Your Capacity?

Three aspects of your experience provide clues to your place on this spectrum.

Maximum milk pumped. One obvious indicator is your pumping history, specifically the most milk you've ever expressed in one sitting. Table 9-1 reflects the experiences of many breastfeeding mothers I have known. It is not based on research, but rather on observation. I hope this can be used as a starting point for others to look at this more scientifically.

	Largest Capacity	Large Capacity	Medium Capacity	Small Capacity	Smallest Capacity
Max milk pumped	10-15 oz. (300-450 mL)	5-9 oz. (150-270 mL)	3-5 oz. (90-150 mL)	2-3 oz. (60-90 mL)	1-2 oz. (30-60 mL)
# feeds/ day	5-6	6-7	7-8	8-9	≥9
Longest stretch	10-12 hr	8-10 hr	8 hr	6-7 hr	4-5 hr

Table 9-1. *Breast Storage Capacity Clues*

Have you ever heard of a mother pumping 10 to 15 oz. (300 to 450 mL) in the morning before her baby awakens? This is one sign of a very large breast storage capacity. Some mothers, on the other hand, pump no more than 3 or 4 oz. (90 to120 mL), even when they feel really full. This is the sign of a medium or small storage capacity.

Feeding pattern. If your maternity leave is at least six weeks long and you're exclusively breastfeeding, you may get a sense of your storage capacity from your baby's feeding pattern. After the first month, if your baby is gaining weight well on fewer than eight feedings per day, this may indicate a large capacity. Another aspect of your baby's feeding pattern that provides a clue is whether your baby usually takes one or both breasts per feeding. Typically, babies take both breasts at least some of the time. But mothers with a large storage capacity often report that their babies are almost always satisfied with just one breast.

Longest stretch between feedings. The breastfed babies who sleep for long stretches at night often have mothers with a large breast storage capacity. That's because with so much room in their milk-making glands, their milk production doesn't slow when their babies sleep for longer than six or seven hours at a time. As a side note, it is common for breastfed babies to wake much more often than every four to five hours when they are hungry. This indicator alone does not tell the whole story.

Your Choices

So where does this leave you in terms of options? Here are some things to consider.

Very large storage capacity. If all the indicators tell you that you probably have a large breast storage capacity, this gives you more options than other mothers. If your capacity is very large, you might be able to work full-time and do what the mother whom I mentioned earlier did. She got up in the morning and pumped milk at home before her baby awakened, which provided most of the milk needed for her work day. Then she breastfed her baby, went to work, and after she returned to her baby at the end of her eight-hour work day, she breastfed again. A pump session shortly after provided the rest of what her baby needed for the next day.

Any size breast storage capacity. The option above will not work for most mothers working full time or long days, so what are some other choices?

- Pump like crazy during your maternity leave and amass a giant freezer stash of milk so that your baby receives your milk for as long as possible after your start back to work.

- Do a partial weaning (see next section) to reduce your milk production enough so you're comfortable during your work day without pumping but can still breastfeed at home. While at work, your baby would receive pumped milk, formula, or both.

- Gradually wean from the breast (see Chapter 13) a couple of weeks before you start back to work, substituting stored milk or formula for feedings.

The choice is completely up to you. When considering your options, keep in mind that breastfeeding doesn't have to be all or nothing. From a health standpoint, there is value to both you and your baby in any amount of nursing.

Staying Comfortable at Work

As mentioned, breast storage capacity can have a huge impact on your comfort at work. The larger your storage capacity, the longer it takes for your breasts to feel full and for your milk production to slow. However, even if your storage capacity is medium or small and your work days long, you still may be able to both breastfeed and stay comfortable.

The Length of Your Work Day

Your comfort and risk of leaking milk are dependent on two main factors, your breast storage capacity and the length of your work day. If your work day is shorter than your longest stretch between feedings at home, you should be able to go back to work without making any changes in your milk supply. Let's say you'll be away from your baby for six hours during your work day, and your baby currently sleeps for six hours at night. If you are comfortable for that six-hour stretch of time, you're good to go. Alternatively, if your time away from your baby is eight hours, and you feel full-to-bursting in the rare cases when you've gone for that long, it's best to make some changes before you return to work.

Would a Partial Weaning Help?

If your work day is longer than your baby's longest stretch between feedings at home and you won't be pumping or breastfeeding at work, consider a partial weaning. It allows you to reduce your milk production enough to avoid full breasts during your work day, yet leaves enough milk so you can breastfeed when you're home. For example, instead of being at full milk production, you might reduce your milk supply by half and breastfeed part time.

How to do a partial weaning. There are different ways to go about this. Here's one:

227

- Note your usual breastfeeding times. About a week or two before returning to work, pick one feeding during the hours you'll be working. (Avoid the first morning feeding when you will likely feel full already.)

- If you have not given formula, and your baby is younger than 12 months, talk to your baby's health care provider about what to substitute for your milk and feed your baby this at the missed breastfeeding.

- Continue feeding this substitute at about the same time each day.

- Give your body at least two to three days before dropping another breastfeeding. If your breasts become full, express just enough milk to feel comfortable and no more. This will slow your milk production gradually, without pain or risk of infection.

- Repeat until you are comfortable without breastfeeding for the entire length of your work day.

Another way to do a partial weaning is to continue offering the breast first at all feedings while you're with your baby and offer the substitute in-between. When your baby regularly takes as much supplement as you would expect him to take during your work day, you are ready.

Quick Tips for an Easier Transition

While you're in the planning stages, consider these strategies to help ease your adjustment back to work.

Scheduling Your Return

When you notify your employer about your return to work, explore the possibility of moving gradually into your ultimate work schedule. Going slower at first may make this adjustment easier for both you and your baby. Here are some approaches.

Work Fewer Hours Per Week

Whether you'll be working full-time or part-time, consider starting back to work at fewer hours per week for as long as is practical. If your work day is normally 8 hours, see if you can arrange to work four hours per day in the beginning. Then move up to 6 hours per day and eventually increase to your full eight-hour work days. Finances and flexibility will no doubt play a role in how this plays out, but even a short ramp-up may smooth out this process as you adjust.

Schedule a Day Off Mid-week

For example, if you work Monday through Friday, arrange for a while to have Wednesdays off. This gives you a break every two days for rest and catch-up breastfeeding.

Start Near the End of the Week

Rather than starting on a Monday with five full work days ahead of you, consider starting back on a Thursday or Friday. You can either combine this with the previous strategies or as an alternative to them. Even if this is the only scheduling change you can make, it is well worth it.

Postpone Your Return

Alison B. from Indiana, USA described how postponing her return to work made a difference.

> Being ready to go back to work and being ready to leave my baby were not the same thing at all. When I planned my maternity leave, I scheduled it for 8 weeks, not really having any idea what that meant. At 6 weeks, I panicked and wrote my boss an email saying that I was postponing my return until 10 weeks, which he thankfully agreed to.

Pump Planning

The following tips may simplify your pumping routine at work and at home.

Your Pump Schedule at Work

No doubt you've already given some thought to your pumping schedule at work. The number of pump sessions per day needed to keep your milk production steady over the long term will depend on your baby's age, your breast storage capacity, the number of hours you and your baby are apart, and whether you plan to provide only your milk for your baby. It will take some time for you to figure out the routine that works best for you, which is covered in detail in the Chapter 11. Until then, however, you need a starting point.

Number of pump sessions at work. To decide how many times to pump at work when you first start back, count how many hours you'll be away from your baby, including travel time. Until you see how your body responds to the changes in routine, try not to go longer than about 3 hours without removing the milk from your breasts. Assuming you'll be breastfeeding as the last thing you do before leaving your baby and the first thing you do when you are reunited, use this plan as a starting point:

- 6 hours apart = 1 pump session (unless your baby is already going for 6-hour stretches between feedings at home)

- 9 hours apart = 2 pump sessions

- 12 hours apart = 3 pump sessions

Time needed per pump session. Most mothers working full-time with young babies pump twice per day and spend less than an hour per day total pumping (Slusser, Lange, Dickson, Hawkes, & Cohen, 2004). Allow at least 20 to 30 minutes per pump session, including clean-up.

Where to store your milk. Depending on the room temperature at work and the length of your work day, you may or may not need to cool your pumped milk. The season and your climate will affect whether or not your milk needs to be cooled while you travel from work to home. As long as you follow the milk storage guidelines in Chapter 6, any milk you store at room temperature can be refrigerated and/or frozen later.

If you need to cool your milk, you have several options:

- Pump bag cooler compartment with freezer packs

- Separate cooler bag with freezer packs

- Private or shared refrigerator

Simplifying Washing

You can eliminate the need to clean your pump parts at work by buying enough extra pieces so that you have enough clean sets for every pump session. According to the experts, there's no benefit to sterilizing pump parts after every use (Jones & Tully, 2011). Normal hygiene is fine. (Remember, your milk has antibacterial properties.)

To clean your parts, first rinse all the pieces with milk on them in cool water, wash them in warm, soapy water, then rinse well. With the right number of clean sets, you can do all of the washing at home. If you have a dishwasher, it can do this work for you.

You don't have to buy multiple "pump kits," which can be expensive. You just need enough of the specific pump parts that are washed after each pumping session. Normally, that would not include the pump tubing or the piece that connects the tubing to the pump motor. It would include the milk container (most pumps with carry bags come with extra bottles or you can use milk freezer bags), the pump pieces you hold to your breasts, and any other parts that the milk touches. These parts can usually be ordered individually online.

Pump Packing and Unpacking at Home

Work days are full of details to remember, especially during the morning rush. In some families, to streamline their routine, the mother's partner takes on the responsibility of unpacking the pump and milk after work, storing the milk, cleaning the parts, and repacking the pump for the next day. If you have a partner and he or she is available and willing to do this, it can be a significant contribution to the breastfeeding relationship. This commitment allows you to focus on your baby when you're at home, while someone else handles these pumping details for you.

Figure 9-2. *One way a mother's partner can support breastfeeding is by taking on the task of unpacking and packing her pump and milk after work.* ©2014 Ameda, Inc. Used with permission.

Work Wardrobe

Before returning to work, think about your wardrobe and how well it fits with your plan to breastfeed or pump. You might also want to consider the following.

- Have breast pads on hand and an extra top available in case of milk leakage. (An alternative is LilyPadz, a silicone product worn inside your bra that applies

234

pressure to your nipples to prevent milk leakage.)

- Wear two-piece outfits, so you can pump or breast-feed without having to fully undress.

- Wear patterned tops rather than solid colors to better camouflage leaks or spilled milk.

- Have a jacket or sweater handy for use as a cover-up if needed.

Now that we've covered many of the practical details of returning to work, it's time to focus on the soft side: your feelings about this major transition and your baby's reaction to your time apart.

10

Your Feelings About Returning to Work

Practical details are important. But feelings are important too. This chapter focuses on the softer side of going back to work: the emotions that go along with it. Mothers' feelings run the gamut, and this chapter covers the entire range. Babies sometimes react to their new back-to-work routine too, most commonly with changes in feeding and sleeping patterns. It can help to know what to expect, and it can most definitely help to know that you're not alone, and where to find the support you need.

What Affects Your Feelings

It's impossible to completely separate your body and your feelings. Both are affected by your return to work.

Physical Recovery

As mentioned in Chapter 1, even 11 weeks postpartum, many women have not fully physically recovered from delivery. As I described earlier, in one study, women at 11 weeks postpartum reported an average of four childbirth-related symptoms, such as pain and fatigue (McGovern et al., 2007). Mothers who had cesarean sections had more health problems than those who delivered vaginally (McGovern et al., 2006). As Melissa M. from New York, USA described in Chapter 3, "Six weeks to go through the most life- and body-changing things was a pittance." If you're returning to work within the first three months, expect that it may take awhile for your energy to return to its normal level.

Lauren J. from New York, USA describes her experience: "My son was only 8 weeks old when I had to return to my full-time job as a clinical social worker. It was a tremendous struggle, both physically and emotionally. I felt as though he and I were just starting to get the hang of this breastfeeding thing, and then I had to leave him."

Range of Emotions

Mothers' feelings about returning to work are understandably mixed and vary tremendously from woman to woman.

What Research Tells Us

To understand more fully mothers' feelings about returning to work, researchers surveyed 74 mothers who were back at their full-time jobs after an average of 10 weeks (Nichols & Roux, 2004). Using open-ended questions, the researchers discovered that while the mothers had a variety of feelings, the negatives outweighed the positives. These were the most common challenges women reported. They:

- Found it difficult to leave their babies,

- Felt pressured by conflicting demands on their time and energy,

- Felt overloaded with work-family stresses,

- Faced childcare and financial pressures, and

- Experienced sleep deprivation and mood changes.

On the positive side, these study mothers also:

- Enjoyed motherhood,

- Learned from this experience how to ask for and receive help,

- Successfully realigned their priorities and lifestyle to better suit their new family dynamics, and

- Derived satisfaction from their work.

Separation Anxiety

The most common challenge the study mothers reported was being separated from their babies. This is not surprising, as a strong emotional attachment to our babies is key to human survival. Rachel F. from Kentucky, USA returned to her full-time job as a public-health counselor at 12 weeks with both of her daughters.

> It doesn't get easier the second time. Both times I didn't want to do it, and both times I cried. Returning to work is one of the hardest things for a mom to experience, in my opinion. When you grow a person inside of you, you instinctively want to remain close to the one who is so dependent on you for everything. Allowing someone else to take care of my girls because I had to work to bring in income for our family was beyond difficult emotionally. I just wanted to be with my babies.

Some mothers find unique ways to cope with this stress. Vivienne M. from Maryland, USA returned to work part time as a software engineer when both of her daughters were 4 months old.

> I was fortunate to be able to telecommute for the first year of their lives, and their caregiver brought them to me when they wanted to feed. (How awesome is that!) When I first returned to work, I remember missing my baby physically and feeling guilty that

she might be upset and I wasn't there to comfort her. During the first couple of weeks at work, I actually searched around the house, and found a soft toy that was roughly the size of my infant. I tucked it inside my shirt, mimicking the kangaroo position where my baby would sleep, and I felt comforted! I'd tell myself that it was OK to work. The baby was sleeping, and well loved and cared for. Not something that you would want to do in an office, but it just was hard to not have my baby with me, especially during those first couple of weeks.

Some mothers have more mixed feelings about being away from their babies. Becca, A. from Tennessee, USA, returned to work at 12 weeks as a full-time project manager for a publishing house.

I felt very torn at first between enjoying getting back to working life and feeling like part of me was far away. Pumping sessions at work were a break in my day to think about my baby. I would look at pictures and watch videos, and it really brightened my mood and made me miss him less because I was taking breaks to focus on him.

However, once back at work, not all mothers miss their babies. Sofiya P., who worked as a part-time legal secretary for a New York City law firm, was able to work from home for a couple of months, returning to the office three days a week when her baby was 4 months old. She felt relieved to be back in the office.

> Is it strange that I was relieved to go back after 4 months at home with my baby? All I wanted to do was get out of the house, put on clothes that weren't stained or smelled like spit up, and do things that did not involve or revolve around my baby. To this day, I wonder if there is something wrong with me that I don't feel sad dropping my boy off at daycare, where I know he is treated well by kids and caretakers alike. I guess I am lucky that I have a "good" baby. He is social and happy most of the time. When I went back to work, we hired a nanny, and he took to her without a second thought. I found it easier to handle two days at home with him rather than the full work week.
>
> I wonder how many mothers actually feel the way I do—happy to be doing their job, to be around other adults in a professional setting. You don't see this kind of mother much in the media. Do I wish that I wanted to be home all the time with him? Sometimes. But that is not my reality.

Factors That May Affect Your Feelings

Every mother is different, and there are many factors that may affect how you feel when you start work. Here are just a few.

- Your job specifics (maternity leave, hours per week, your feelings about your work)

- Your mood and adjustment to motherhood

- Whether your baby is easy, challenging, or in between

Let's look at these factors one by one.

Your job specifics. Many aspects of your job can affect how you feel about returning to it. Does your employer offer much flexibility? Can you leave work at your workplace, or do you have to bring work home? Did you choose to work, or do you have to work? Here are some other factors that may affect your feelings.

A longer maternity leave, as mentioned in Chapter 1, usually makes returning to work easier (Ogbuanu, Glover, Probst, Liu, & Hussey, 2011). You have more time to physically recover from childbirth, your baby outgrows the fussy periods that are so common during early infancy, and your months at home make it easier for you and your baby to form a solid bond. Yet a longer maternity leave is no guarantee that you'll feel 100% positive when the time comes to return to work. Michelle P. from Newfoundland, Canada returned to work full-time as a newspaper reporter when her younger daughter was 10 months old.

How did I feel? I felt anxious at first. I wasn't sure how it was going to work out. I dreaded it, honestly. But very quickly I came to feel lucky. At that time,

243

the chaos of two kids at different ages was overwhelming and I was glad to leave that behind for the peace of the office for stretches at a time. I could phone to hear about what was going on and as time went on I really enjoyed the rhythm.

Fionnuala M. from Ireland, a full-time communications manager for a charity, returned to work when her son was 10 months old.

He is my third baby, and I had already worked and breastfed once so I knew I could do it. I knew that my son would survive, but I was worried about how he would manage without the comfort, especially in a new environment. It felt odd to expect him to make such a big adjustment without his daily comfort. Emotionally, I felt a bit conflicted because I wanted to return to work but didn't want to leave my baby, and I was worried about the amount of juggling involved.

Crystal N., a full-time public-health nurse from Manitoba, Canada, returned to work full-time as a public-health nurse when the youngest of her three daughters was 12 months old.

It was very hard to go back after a full year of getting to spend every day with them. I wasn't ready to go back full-time. I felt like I had worked so hard to establish this great breastfeeding team between me and my LO and I couldn't believe it was coming to an end.

The hours per week you work may also influence your feelings. As described in Chapter 2, on average, mothers who work part time breastfeed as long as mothers who are not employed (Ogbuanu, Glover, Probst, Hussey, & Liu, 2011). Working full-time means more hours apart, which often means more breastfeeding challenges. Melissa M. from New York, USA returned to work full-time as an education-claims processor for the U.S. Department of Veterans Affairs when her son was 6 weeks and 6 days old.

> It was the hardest thing I have ever done. I felt guilty, sad, depressed and without choice. I cried after dropping off, I cried through work, through pumping, and I counted the hours to get back to him. I worked 45 to 50 hours a week when he was tiny. I gave up and went back to refusing overtime as he got older. I didn't want to miss everything to the babysitter/daycare center.

How you feel about your job can also make a difference. If you love your work, you'll probably feel more positively about going back. It's okay to love your baby and your job. Marge G. from Ohio, USA returned to her obstetric practice part time seven weeks after her son Dan was born.

> Dan was nursing well, the pumping was going fine, and I was dying to get back to my "normal life." I

loved breastfeeding, and of course I loved my son, but I am not a baby person (funny thing for an OB to say but you know what I mean) and it was so hard being home all day and pacing myself for a baby. I was ready to go back to seeing patients. Fortunately, I had a private administrative office, and my schedule was very flexible, especially since my practice had dwindled while I was out. I blocked out 1.5 hours for lunch/pumping every day around 1 pm, and I could double pump enough for all his feedings during my work day. I was proud of nursing. The breastfeeding and providing all his milk made me feel connected, a 24/7 mother.

Your mood and your adjustment to motherhood. How well you adjust to motherhood and whether you suffer from postpartum depression are likely to affect your feelings too. Karen C. from California, USA worked part time as a technical researcher for an aerospace firm. She describes how her difficult emotional adjustment to motherhood with her first baby affected her feelings about returning to work and how that changed with her second baby.

With my first baby, I couldn't wait to return to work at 4.5 months. My transition to motherhood was difficult emotionally. I felt like a failure as a mother, breastfeeding was a struggle, and she was a higher-needs baby. I looked forward to leaving her with the caregiver that I had worked hard to find, and felt immensely relieved to have three days a week without the stress of being her mother. I noticed that a few hours away from her during the day allowed me the space I needed to let my emotions catch up, and after a few months back at work I began to feel much more bonded than I had before I returned to work. Now she is 4, and I miss her tremendously when we're apart.

My second baby was nothing but joy, an easy birth, natural nurser, an easy-going, happy baby. I dreaded my return to work, also at 4.5 months, and where I had handed my daughter off without a thought, I lingered and lingered at his first drop-off. I missed him terribly.

Depression not only affects a mother's feelings, it can also affect her relationship with her baby and her partner. Joy S. from Kentucky, USA went back to work full-time as a project manager assistant for a general contracting company when her son was 2 months old.

I had a hard time with returning to work. I suffered from postpartum depression, and going back to work did not help. Before he was born, we made the decision that my husband would be a stay-at-home dad. The decision was mainly based on financial reasons. I would have rather been the stay-at-home parent, but I knew logically that this was the best decision for us. My emotions, on the other hand, didn't get that memo! I dealt with jealousy of my husband spending all that time with our son. I felt I was better equipped to be at home and had a hard time letting my husband do things his way. He is a great father and does a great job, but emotionally, it was hard not being at home. It has been an ongoing process of checking my attitude and reminding myself to be thankful that every day I am leaving my son with his father.

An easy or challenging baby. The baby we give birth to is not always the baby we expect. Julianne W. from Connecticut, USA found going back to work hard in part because her daughter Addie was so colicky, which made early motherhood a struggle for her.

For as long as I could remember, I wanted to be a mother. But Addie screamed almost constantly for the first three months of her life. She didn't latch well, didn't sleep well, and generally seemed to hate everything, including me. It was so frustrating and difficult, I cried almost constantly for three months along with her and felt like such a failure. I knew motherhood wouldn't be a walk in a park, but I just wanted to hide in my room or hand Addie over to someone who could obviously do so much better than I was doing. So when returning to work finally came around, I thought it would be pure relief to return to the world of normal volume levels and feeling competent.

But being at work while my husband was at home with a screaming child was terrible for a good while.

My husband and I would talk throughout the day and he would tell me how bad the day was going, how cranky Addie was, how she hadn't napped well. This made me feel as if he resented being home (he had worked in a fast-paced office before we moved) and resented me working, even though in his mind, he was simply reporting on the day. The guilt I felt was crippling, causing me to be distracted at work, depressed, and angry with my husband.

For the first month or two after I returned to work, Addie would be screaming when I came home and it was so jarring after a relatively peaceful day that I would take extra time cleaning up my pump parts, stowing my milk, cleaning up the house, and changing my clothes before I could pick her up and say hello. I'm not terribly proud of that, and it made me feel like an even worse mother, especially once my husband realized what was going on and called me out on it. But I also knew that once I was home, I would shoulder 100% of the Addie responsibility as my husband felt like he had already put in his time and it was my turn. And certainly I would want to cuddle up with my child after being away from her all day, right? Yes, but not for the four solid hours before bedtime of screaming, walking around holding her, and feeling once again like a terrible mother who could do no right. And I knew I would sleep with Addie and nurse her several times during the night. It was hard after a draining day at work to be further drained.

Once Addie stopped screaming so much (around 4 or 5 months) and started smiling and interacting, she wanted to be with my husband much more than me, and that really hurt. He's brilliant with her and she adores him for it. It seemed she really only wanted me for milk. I couldn't soothe her when she was crying, or play with her and make her giggle. Then I really felt like a failure, and I was angry with my husband, as if he were turning her against me on purpose. Only recently has she started giving equal "giggle time" and smiles to both mommy and daddy, and I've found ways to soothe her that are my own.

My husband and I are still working through it, and there are still some really bad days. Now that Addie wants to interact, I'm finding new ways to connect with her beyond nursing. It's still hard for me to reconcile my reality with what I thought motherhood would be and feel good about it, but I think we're all finding our groove and figuring out how to be a functional, happier family.

How you feel about your mothering competence (as Julianne's story above illustrates so well) also affects your feelings when you return to work. Your confidence as a mother can be very different with your first baby than with your second. Emily H. from Illinois, USA had her first child when she was 18, just 6 weeks before she started as a full-time college student and began a 20-hour-per-week part-time job. As a first-time mother, she was reluctant to ask for what she needed, which changed with her second baby.

> Initially, it was hard. I wasn't quite sure how to make everything work, and I felt guilty and inadequate. I only breastfed my son for about three months, because I didn't pump consistently and my milk supply dropped. Breastfeeding was much easier the second time.
>
> My daughter was born during the fall semester when I was 20, and I took her to my classes. I was pursuing my bachelor's degree in early childhood. Because of my child-development background, I was determined to breastfeed for at least a year. I breastfed on demand for four months, when she started childcare and I returned to work. My milk supply was much more established than it had been with my son, and I was more determined when I returned to my part-time student job. I don't remember feeling guilty as I had with my son. I only felt a determination to ensure I breastfed as long as possible.
>
> I pumped consistently. I was very open with my coworkers, even using a coworker's office to pump during the day. I also was very open with complete strangers. At one point, I had to find another place on campus to pump. I walked into an office filled with women, explained my situation, and they pro-

vided me a place to pump when I needed it. I only had to walk into their office and pick up a key.

My first experience with breastfeeding and returning to work was full of disappointment and guilt. I learned from that experience. I was more educated, had more determination, and was successful the second time around.

Breastfeeding Support

Emily's story illustrates how important support can be. One way to reduce the stress of early motherhood and returning to work is to reach out to others. Friends, family, and coworkers may provide support. If you have people in your life who have breastfed as long as you intend to, that's a wonderful thing! But even if you do, there are also other excellent sources of breastfeeding support, both in-person and online. Joy S. from Kentucky, USA, who had suffered with postpartum depression, found breastfeeding-support meetings made a huge difference to her.

> I found and joined a La Leche League group that is a couple of towns over and they have been a tremendous help. There are other working/pumping moms and we compare notes and swap stories. I wish I had found them when I was going through the rough patch, but am very grateful to have them now. I find that I am helping other mothers as much

as they are helping me! A good support group goes a very long way!

Breastfeeding support comes in many forms in this digital age. A great resource is Lara Audelo's book, *The Virtual Breastfeeding Culture*. For details on how to contact online and in-person breastfeeding support organizations, see the Resources section.

Figure 10-1. *It feels so good to have someone to turn to who has been there, done that.*

Changing Your Mind

Every other section of this book assumes that you will follow through on your plans to return to work, and in many families, that is a given. In 2010, almost 41% of the babies born in the U.S. were born to single mothers (CDC, 2013). And in 2013, women were the sole or primary breadwinner in 40% of U.S. households (Wang, Parker, & Taylor, 2013).

However, in some cases, women who fully intended to go back to work after the birth of their baby don't. And sometimes those who think they'll be going back to work full-time find another path. Jennifer E. from California, USA, a registered nurse, thought at first that she would be her family's sole wage-earner after her baby's birth, but then things changed.

> My husband and I always knew one of us was going to stay home with our daughter, even before we got pregnant. My husband had not found steady work in construction and I had a great job as a registered nurse at a prominent health care organization in San Diego. After becoming pregnant, I had an immense desire to move back to our home town, 5 hours north of San Diego. Because my husband couldn't find a job that justified the move, I had to find a job that allowed us to move.
>
> It only took a week to get the new job, and I was four months pregnant already. I worked for this physician for four months, the whole time reassuring them that I was definitely coming back to work after my four-month maternity leave. I was confident that I would have no problem leaving the baby with my husband, and he would have both of our mothers around just in case he needed extra help those first few weeks.

After my daughter was born, there was a lot of tension in the house regarding our agreed arrangement. Figuring out when to pump, how to get the baby to take a bottle, and when to introduce the bottle were all issues I thought about regularly. My husband started to feel uneasy about staying home with the baby, and we constantly looked for jobs for him so that I might be able to stay home. I knew I ultimately always wanted to be the one to stay home with our children, but because the job market wasn't great for construction, I knew I was going to have to make do.

Then I went to work. My daughter was 3 months old, and I was only going to have to go to work for two days then I would have a long weekend before starting my normal schedule. The whole time I was at work, I couldn't enjoy myself. I could do my job, but it was difficult to be happy, and I think it showed. My husband started considering joining the military in order to provide for us. He was willing to be deployed in order to provide for our family. I wasn't very comfortable with that idea, but it was a relief of sorts for both of us to admit that we wanted to switch places. Up until this time we had acted so confident in our plan, but we were fooling ourselves.

I felt so much better going to work knowing I wouldn't have to go much longer. Ultimately I was fired the day I gave notice at work, and I was so glad

I didn't have to go through with the rest of my work schedule. We scrambled to get my husband a job, because the military process was long and we had just got it started. He worked for my father doing farm labor for months, and in the end we decided the military would separate us too much for it to be worth it.

Within four months, my husband had three job offers in his chosen field. Ultimately, it has worked out perfectly for us, and we are so satisfied and happy with our choice. The dynamic between us was instantly better when we switched roles, and we have never questioned our current situation, even though I would have been making a lot more money than my husband.

Kim S. from Virginia, USA served full-time in the U.S. Navy after her first child was born, but made a different choice after she had her second baby.

It's not that I didn't want to stop working sooner. I had to wait until the end of my Navy contract. My mother was watching my son so it wasn't dissatisfaction with daycare. I just wanted to spend time with him. When I was ready for a second baby, that's when I dropped my paperwork. The daycare possibility made me nervous. And since I breastfeed, it has been wonderful to not have to worry much about pumping and bottles.

Elizabeth J from North Carolina, USA was 40 with a full-time job as a crisis-line coordinator and counselor at a local domestic-violence agency when she found out she was pregnant. During her pregnancy, she went through an identity crisis and realized she needed to quit her full-time job and eventually started her own part-time business.

It took me almost the entire nine months of my pregnancy to realize that quitting my job was the right thing to do. I'm an intensely loyal person and I loved my work. But the agency was going through a merger and the powers-that-be couldn't tell me what my job would be post-merger. Also, my job was more than full time and to say that it was a huge emotional life suck is an understatement. I gave six-weeks' notice. My last day was 1 month before I was due.

My work has always been important to me, and I couldn't conceive of wanting to be home with our daughter full time. So my plan after leaving my position was to start looking for a full-time job in an alternate field. I was ready to go to an interview when it hit me that I was going to interview for jobs that I didn't care that much about, just because it was decent pay and also because it felt like something that I "should" do. This "should" was grounded in my past identify as someone who works as a professional. When I realized that, I cancelled that interview and called off that search.

I reached out instead to a mentor and said I was looking for very part-time work in any field. She hooked me up with someone looking for help staffing a new upscale shoe boutique. It sounded like a good fit: close by, flexible, pay almost what I was paid in my old job (seriously) and best of all, it wasn't emotionally taxing. I took the job.

At the same time I learned about postpartum doulas and decided it was the path for me. I have always worked supporting women and this seemed another way that just made sense. Over the next year, I started to make sense of my new identity as a person who is someone's mother but still "me."

It became about more than wanting to offer support and help, I realized that we moms need to give ourselves permission to count again. I needed to. We're still important as individuals with needs, even if we are someone's mom. And so a metamorphosis from "just" postpartum doula services to what is now the new business I'm about to launch, where I help new and expecting moms start good habits early by making their needs as important as their partners', babies' or other kids.'

Your Baby's Responses

It's not just mothers who sometimes have strong feelings about their return to work. Depending on temperament, babies sometimes do too. Don't be surprised if your baby begins waking more at night, breastfeeds more often, or is fussier than usual soon after you start work. If this happens, think about how you would like to be treated during a major life change.

If a baby's sleep or feeding pattern changes, some of the mothers I've helped have been told by well-meaning friends, relatives and even health care providers to just let their babies cry. A kinder, gentler strategy during any stressful time is to give your baby extra holding, skin-to-skin contact, and reassurance. Kimberly P. from Texas, USA, a full-time teacher, found that after she started work, her son fed more often after she got home.

> My son was 4.5 months old when I went back to the classroom and he was resilient. It didn't seem to bother him to be away from me much of the day. He enjoyed his caregiver, played with the other children, and never cried when I left him or picked him up. He nursed more frequently at night and on the weekends, and he had his share of colds, but he was (and is) a happy, well-adjusted little guy.

Rachel F. from Kentucky, USA, a full-time public-health counselor, returned to work when her daughters were 12 weeks old. When she started back to work with her second daughter, her baby's feeding patterns changed drastically.

My first daughter adjusted well to daycare. With my second daughter, my husband was working from home, but she didn't adjust as well to being separated from me. She wouldn't take a bottle during the day and essentially only drank 1 to 1.5 oz. (30 to 45 mL) of breast milk the whole time I was away until my husband introduced a sippy cup to her at 5 months of age. She did much better with that than the bottle. She also reverse cycled most feeds at night when I returned to work, waking up four to six times each night, so on top of feeling sad to be away from her, I was also exhausted each and every day.

Michelle F. from British Columbia, Canada, a full-time registered nurse, returned to work when her son was 15 months old. He showed some signs of stress through unusual bouts of fussiness, which she responded to with love and affection.

He adapted well to the babysitter. After two weeks of crying when I left, he stopped and welcomed her with open arms. There were times when he was unexplainably fussy or in need of extra love and affection, which my husband and I doled out happily.

The next chapter focuses on your return to work, with a focus on how to tailor your daily routine to keep your milk production steady, and approaches to night feedings that can help you get more rest.

11

Back to Work: Keeping Milk Production Stable

This chapter describes what you need to know after returning to work to meet your long-term breastfeeding goals. It explains which of the many day-to-day details are key and which you can ignore. And it explains how your baby's sleep patterns—a hot topic for any parent—can affect the big picture. Knowledge is power, and hopefully the information here will help you make decisions with confidence.

A Vulnerable Time

When you make plans for your first month at work, consider this a vulnerable time, especially if you have a small baby. As you begin working, be very kind to yourself. One study found that mothers who returned to work when their babies were younger than 6 months were more than twice as likely to stop breastfeeding during their first month back compared with mothers not yet on the job (Kimbro, 2006).

Chapter 9 described strategies for easing this transition. But even if you use all of those tips, this major change won't necessarily be easy. Just like after giving birth, this is a good time to take advantage of all offers of help, keep your focus on what's important, and simplify your life as much as possible.

Wendy R. from Texas, USA returned to work full-time at 7 weeks and learned from that experience.

> I didn't have all the knowledge that I do now...I would encourage moms to try their best to take off as long as possible from work. This time is precious and you never get it back. If working is an absolute must, then be careful to de-stress your life in every other way possible. Working outside the home and being a new mom and pumping is crazy enough all in itself without adding every other facet of life. Slow down.

Eat Well

One way to take care of yourself is to avoid skipping meals and eat healthy foods. Unless it's extreme, your diet is unlikely to affect how much milk you make or its quality. But eating healthy helps keep up your energy and your resistance to illness during this busy time.

Some mothers wonder what to eat when their work meal breaks are spent pumping. In Chapter 5, hands-free pumping options were mentioned. But if you're trying to pump one-handed, here are some ideas of healthy foods you can eat with one hand while you pump.

- Your favorite sandwich

- Hard-boiled eggs with a handful of cherry tomatoes

- Slices of turkey rolled-up with a handful of grapes

- A rice cake with cheese spread

Many more practical and nutritious finger foods are listed in the "Making It Work for Moms" brochure at: *http://www.breastfeedingpartners.org/images/pdf/ForMomsFINAL.pdf*.

Understand Basic Dynamics

Worry about milk production is the single biggest concern breastfeeding mothers mention. But being employed and breastfeeding can elevate this from a concern to an obsession. Plus, it doesn't help if you find yourself being regaled with stories of employed mothers who failed to keep their milk flowing.

To meet your goals, you need to understand the basic dynamics of milk production, which were explained in detail in Chapter 3. But more than that, you need to know the impact of your daily routine on these dynamics. I hope my "magic number" concept will remove some of the mystery around milk supply and help you keep your focus on the big picture as you sort out the details (Mohrbacher, 2011).

The Magic Number

Every breastfeeding mother has a magic number. Your magic number is the number of daily milk removals (breast-feeds plus pumps) needed to keep your supply steady over time. To estimate your magic number, think about how many times during the last week or two of your maternity leave that your baby breastfed each day. This may be close to your magic number if all of the following are true:

- Your maternity leave was at least six weeks long.

- You breastfed on cue rather than on a fixed schedule.

- Your exclusively breastfed baby gained weight well.

After returning to work, the key to keeping your milk production steady over the long term is for your number of daily milk removals to stay at or above your magic number. To understand this better, here's a quick review of the two main milk-production dynamics.

Breast Fullness and Milk Production

You may remember from Chapter 3 that breast fullness determines how fast or slow you make milk. "Drained breasts make milk faster and full breasts make milk slower" describes this dynamic. The fuller your breasts become, the slower you make milk. The opposite is also true. Milk production speeds when your breasts are drained more fully. At an average breastfeeding, your baby takes about two-thirds of your milk and leaves one-third. To increase your milk supply as needed, your baby feeds more often and for a longer time, taking a larger percentage of your available milk. This happens naturally when you're with your baby and feeding on cue. You don't even need to think about it. Just let nature take its course.

When you return to work, however, if your baby no longer has access to your breasts around the clock, this means you need to start paying attention. Your milk supply is no longer naturally regulated by your baby.

Why Magic Numbers Vary

Mothers have different magic numbers in part because they have different breast storage capacities. Breast storage capacity refers to the amount of milk available in your breasts when they're at their fullest time of the day. Storage capacity is not about breast size, which is determined mostly by the amount of fatty tissue in your breasts. It is based on the amount of room within your milk-making glands. Smaller-breasted mothers can have a large capacity and larger-breasted mothers can have a small capacity.

Differences in storage capacity account for much of the variations among breastfed babies' feeding patterns:

- Whether your baby usually takes one breast or both.

- Number of daily feedings needed for your baby to gain weight.

- Your baby's longest sleep stretch.

Both large-capacity and small-capacity mothers produce plenty of milk. But their babies feed differently to get the milk they need.

A mother with a large storage capacity has more room in her breasts, so it takes more milk (and more time) for the pressure in her full breasts to build to the point that milk production slows. With more milk available, her baby may always be satisfied with one breast. As he gets older, he may gain weight well with fewer feedings per day than the average baby. And, he may sleep for longer stretches at night than most babies without milk production slowing. The magic number of the mother with a large storage capacity is likely to be lower—maybe only five or six milk removals per day—than the magic number of the mother with a medium or small breast storage capacity.

The mother with a small storage capacity has less milk available at each feeding. Her baby may want both breasts more often, need more daily feedings to get the same amount of milk, and wake more often at night to feed, even as he gets older. Because she has less room for milk in her breasts, they will get full enough for milk production to slow sooner than the mother with a medium or large capacity. If the baby of the small-capacity mother sleeps too long, his mother's breasts quickly become so full of milk that her production slows. A small-capacity mother's magic number will likely be higher—maybe eight or nine milk removals per day—than the mother with a medium or large storage capacity. (The magic number of the average mother is around seven or eight milk removals per day.)

For an idea of where you might fall on the breast-storage-capacity spectrum, see Table 9-1 in Chapter 9, which lists several signs that provide clues. You may find it helpful to have a general idea of your magic number, so that you have a starting point from which to plan your daily routine after you return to work.

How to Use Your Magic Number

Your magic number can help you establish a routine that keeps your milk supply steady over the long haul. Rather than basing your schedule on averages or on someone else's experience (whose magic number may be very different from yours), you can tailor your plan to your own body's response.

Because you'll be starting back to work with only an estimate of your magic number, expect that you might need to make adjustments over time. If your estimate is low and your milk production begins to drop, for example, count how many times each 24 hours you're removing milk from your breasts (breastfeeds plus pumps). Your dip in supply tells you that either your number of milk removals is below your magic number or there's an issue with how effectively your pump or your baby is removing your milk. (For example, a baby with a head cold or an ear infection may have trouble nursing for a short time.)

If you've fallen below your magic number, you can reverse this trend by increasing your number of daily milk removals. The sooner you add more milk removals, the sooner you should see improvement. Staying at your magic number should hold your milk production steady. Boosting your daily milk removals above your magic number should increase your supply (for more, see Chapter 12). Your body's response will tell you what you need to know.

Impact of Daily Routines

Your daily routine can make a big difference in your long-term milk production. During the years I helped employed mothers by phone, I began to notice a pattern.

Role of Breastfeeding

Many of the mothers I spoke with who had dropping milk supplies were pumping the recommended number of times at work, but as the months passed, they breastfed fewer and fewer times at home. Many of these women working full-time, for example, were pumping two-to-three times at work but were only breastfeeding two or three times at home. Some were down to four-to-six total milk removals per day from an average of seven or eight when they were on leave. Most often it was the decrease in breastfeeding that caused them to slip below their magic number and their milk production to slow.

Why did this happen? Many of these mothers were applying bottle-feeding norms to a breastfeeding baby. Many were told that as their babies grew bigger and heavier, they should feed fewer times per day, so they began cutting back. This is common with many bottle-feeding babies, who may consume as much as 7 or 8 oz. (210-240 mL) per feeding. But as Chapter 7 described, breastfeeding patterns differ greatly from bottle-feeding patterns. Science tells us that in breastfed babies between 1 and 6 months of age, the volume of milk per feeding and the number of feedings per day doesn't vary by much (Kent et al., 2013). We also know that in part because of these differences, breastfed babies are more likely to have healthier eating habits and weight, while bottle-fed babies are at increased risk of overweight and obesity (Li, Magadia, Fein, & Grummer-Strawn, 2012).

What happens when a breastfeeding mother tries to adopt a bottle-feeding pattern? If her breast storage capacity isn't large enough to sustain it, over time it may cause a decrease in milk production that can lead to slow weight gain or the need to use more and more formula as her pump sessions yield less and less milk. Margarita's experience is a good example of this.

Margarita called me because she was in a quandary. She had been breastfeeding her daughter Luisa for six months, but had been struggling with her milk production since she was 3 months old. Luisa was a sleepy baby from the start and had slept long 10-to-12-hour stretches at night. At first, she breastfed 8-to-10 times per day, and Margarita knew this was normal for a newborn.

But Margarita heard that she should cut back on feedings as Luisa got older. So when she started work at two months, she began to breastfeed less. Almost immediately, her milk production dropped. She started getting up at night to pump because she didn't want to wake her sleeping baby. For a month, she gave her this extra milk during the day and was able to continue to exclusively breastfeed. But as she dropped more feedings, she also dropped the nightly pumping. By 4 months, Margarita was pumping twice at work and breastfeeding three times at home. Her daily total was now five milk removals per day, down from 8 to 10 when she was home. Luisa needed more milk than she could pump at work, so she began giving her formula as well.

Margarita tried some of the milk-increasing tips she had heard about (see the next chapter). For a while, she took three capsules of the herb fenugreek three times per day, and later her doctor prescribed metoclopramide, a drug that increases milk production in some women. When she did this, her milk production would increase. But when she stopped, her production slowed again.

I explained to Margarita how breast fullness and milk storage capacity affect milk production, and she realized that she had a medium storage capacity. She also now understood what was going wrong. Her strategy of dropping feedings as Luisa grew older was working against her.

She had a breastfeeding goal of one year, and she still wanted to achieve it. What did she do? She increased her number of breastfeeding sessions at home and pumping sessions at work and started pumping right before she went to bed. (She could have done "dream feeds" with Luisa at night—nursing her while she was still half-asleep—but she decided she'd rather pump.) Meeting her breastfeeding goal was important to her, and now that she knew how to reach it, she adjusted her routine to make it happen.

More Breastfeeding Means Less Pumping

Another important dynamic to keep in mind is that that cutting back on breastfeeding at home means your baby will need more expressed milk while you're at work, which you have to work harder to pump. As described in Chapter 9, your baby needs on average about 30 oz. (900 mL) of milk per day. The more milk your baby gets directly from you, the less milk you need to express. And anything that cuts down on your need to pump is a good thing.

"...cutting back on breastfeeding at home means your baby will need more expressed milk while you're at work..."

The opposite is true too. The less milk your baby gets from the breast, the more milk you'll need to leave for her while you're at work. What's important to a baby is not how much milk she gets at each feeding, but how much milk she gets over the 24-hour day.

Another way to look at this is that breastfed babies average 3 to 4 oz. (90-120 mL) per feeding. For every breastfeeding you drop, your baby needs another 3 to 4 oz. (90-120 mL) while you're at work.

Ways to Fit in More Breastfeeding

After you return to work, what can you do to encourage more breastfeeding? You have several options.

- **Cluster feedings together before you leave for work.** If you leave in the morning, breastfeed twice: once when you wake up and again right before you leave baby. (If baby is asleep, wake her to feed, or do a "dream feed," so she is full when you leave.)

- **Consider nursing midday.** Can you go to your baby for one or more feedings during your work day or have your baby brought to you for breastfeeding?

- **Breastfeed as soon as you and baby are reunited after work.** If she seems hungry just before you arrive, suggest the caregiver give as little milk as possible until you get there.

- **Cluster feedings together when you're home after work.**

- **Nurse before your bedtime.** If your baby goes to sleep for the night earlier than you, do a "dream feed" right before you go to bed, and if your baby sleeps for very long stretches at night, do another you if you awaken during the night.

Figure 11-1. *One breastfeeding in the middle of your work day means one less pump session, which is always a plus.*

Babies can be coaxed to "dream feed" when they're in a light sleep, which you can recognize because you'll see movement, such as eyes moving under eyelids. If you lean back and lay your lightly sleeping baby on top of you, this will trigger her feeding reflexes, and she may start to root. Amazingly, babies don't have to be awake to breastfeed effectively.

Your Pump Schedule and Your Magic Number

Many mothers assume when they go back to work that they need to pump the same number of times or the same time of day that they had been breastfeeding at home. That's not actually necessary. To keep your milk production steady, plan to stay at or above your magic number. But the exact times you pump or breastfeed are not crucial. If possible, try to avoid going longer than seven or eight hours between milk removals (full breasts make milk slower), but other than that, you have the freedom to structure your day in the way that makes most sense for your unique situation.

Your breastfeeding pattern also plays a role. Nora C. from Ontario, Canada shared her experience after she started work full-time: "I returned to work when my son was just under 6 months. He wouldn't take pumped milk at all during the day, so I just breastfed about five or six times before I went to bed (4 pm, 5 pm, 6 pm, 7-8 pm, and 10:30 pm or so) and twice in the morning before work (5:30 am and 7:15 am)."

Breastfeeding Times	Longest Stretches	Comments
5:30 a.m.	7:15 a.m.-4 p.m.	* Seven breastfeeds/
7:15 a.m.	(8 hr., 45 min.)	day are enough
4 p.m.		* But full breasts make
5 p.m.	10:30 p.m.-5:30	milk slower, so Nora
6 p.m.	a.m. (7 hr.)	should shorten her
7-8 p.m.		longest stretch to ≤7
10:30 p.m.		hr. with one mid-work
		pump or breastfeed

Table 11-1. *Nora's Daily Routine, Medium Breast Storage Capacity*

Nora breastfed seven times each day, which—since she had a medium breast storage capacity—would probably be enough to keep her production stable without any pumping at work except for that nearly nine-hour stretch during her work day. To keep her milk supply steady, one option would be to pump once in the middle of her work day so her very full breasts did not make milk slower. Another option was for her caregiver to bring her baby to her to breastfeed (or for Nora to go to her baby) during her longest break (Table 11-1).

Your pumping plan should take your magic number into account. How? Plan to pump the minimum number of times at work needed to both provide the milk you'd like to leave for your baby and to maintain your production. If you have a large storage capacity, you will likely pump more milk at a session than other mothers, so that factors into the equation too. If you haven't yet determined your breast storage capacity, review again Table 9-1 in Chapter 9 and see where you might fall on this spectrum.

As mentioned before, if you have a very large breast storage capacity, your magic number will probably be five or six. If your baby breastfeeds four times when you're together, this means two pumps at work should be enough to keep milk production stable. (Or you could do five breastfeeds at home and one pump at work.) On the other hand, if you have a small storage capacity, your magic number may be eight or nine. If your baby breastfeeds only four times at home, you would need to pump four or five times at work, which would be impractical for most women. Instead, for most it would make far more sense to breastfeed more at home. By breastfeeding six or seven times each day at home, you would be able to keep your milk flowing well with only two pump sessions at work.

Sleep and Night Feedings

With a clear understanding of how milk production works, you can appreciate why night feedings can be such an important part of meeting your breastfeeding goals.

- The number of milk removals over 24 hours regulates milk production.

- Allowing your breasts to stay too full for too long causes milk production to slow.

- Going for very long stretches without breastfeeding when you're at home makes it more challenging to keep your milk removals at or above your magic number.

- Long stretches without breastfeeding at home also means you need to leave more pumped milk for your baby while you're at work.

What is a "very long stretch?" Going six or seven hours is unusual in a breastfeeding baby, but that is not long enough to cause milk production to slow in most women. However, stretches as long as eight-to-12 hours are a real challenge for many.

The Dilemma

In Western countries, parents feel a strong social pressure for their babies to sleep for long stretches at night. One mother I spoke to shows how this can play out. Tawana was on her maternity leave and was preparing to go back to work soon. Her baby, Clevon, was about 6 weeks old. Like most new mothers, she was often asked how many hours her baby slept at night. Tawana discovered that if she put Clevon in a swing, as long as it kept moving, he would stay asleep the entire night (sleeping in a swing is not recommended for safety reasons). But Tawana didn't want to put the swing in her bedroom, because its noise would keep her partner awake. And she didn't want to leave her baby alone while in motion all night in the swing. When I spoke to her, she was sleeping on the sofa in the living room next to her baby's swing and getting up every hour to check on him. Clevon's weight gain had slowed during the week or two he had spent his nights in the swing.

After asking Tawana some questions, it seemed clear that she had a small-to-medium breast storage capacity and such long stretches between milk removals had reduced her milk supply, causing the slowed weight gain. Also, she was exhausted from getting up every hour all night. When Tawana realized that using the swing to keep her baby asleep longer was the root cause of both her exhaustion and her milk-production issues, she decided it made more sense for her baby to sleep in her room and to breastfeed at night again. In her case, her baby's long sleep stretch had led to problems, and she decided to stop making his uninterrupted sleep her top priority.

Many mothers hope their baby will "sleep through the night" during the early months. It is not unusual for some breastfed babies (even newborns) to have one four-to-five-hour sleep stretch, and that is fine. But if your baby sleeps longer than about seven hours and your breast storage capacity is small or medium, as Tawana found, it can lead to milk production issues. This is not something you normally need to worry about while you're on leave, because if milk production slows, your baby naturally breastfeeds more often to boost it again. But in Tawana's case, the moving swing had blunted her baby's natural feeding cues. One of the risks of overusing devices like swings and pacifiers is that they can delay and even eliminate some feedings, which can lower milk production.

There is a natural tension between the Western cultural pressure to encourage babies to sleep for long stretches at night and the importance of frequent milk removal to milk production. Continuing regular night feedings may be important to reaching your breastfeeding target. Yet no one questions the fact that you also need your rest, especially when you're expected to be productive at your job. How do you reconcile these seemingly opposite needs?

Getting the Rest You Need

Fatigue is a normal part of new parenthood, no matter how a baby is fed. During your leave, one way to make up for lost sleep is to sleep when your baby sleeps. That's not possible, though, once you're back at work. So what do you do? First, let's look at two common misconceptions.

Giving formula or bottles at night may actually mean less sleep. It may seem logical that you would get more sleep if you feed your baby formula before bed or if someone else handles some of the night feedings. But research found that mothers who breastfeed around the clock get between 25 and 45 more minutes of sleep, spend more time in deeper sleep, and feel less tired than mixed-feeding or for-mula-feeding mothers (Blyton, Sullivan, & Edwards, 2002; Doan, Gardiner, Gay, & Lee, 2007; Kendall-Tackett, Cong, & Hale, 2011).

Although babies fed formula do seem to sleep more, their mothers don't. The Doan study suggested this is be-cause mothers' sleep is disrupted when others handle night feedings. The Kendall-Tackett study found that the breast-feeding mothers reported more total sleep time and took less time to get back to sleep. In the Blyton study, sleep re-searchers analyzed the brain waves of women during sleep and found that exclusively breastfeeding mothers spent more time in deeper sleep than exclusively formula-feeding mothers and women without infants. It may be that the hor-mones released during breastfeeding improve sleep quality and the more you breastfeed, the better you sleep.

Solid foods don't increase a baby's sleep time. The popular belief that solid foods will help babies sleep longer actually has no basis in fact. In one study, about the same number of babies began sleeping more at night whether they received solid foods or not (Macknin, Medendorp, & Maier, 1989). Sleeping longer at night is a developmental milestone that is unrelated to solid foods.

So if giving formula and solids won't mean more sleep, what *can* you do?

Keep your baby nearby at night. Keeping baby close is key.

The less you have to move around at night to breastfeed, the easier it is to get back to sleep. This can also be a lifesaver for your baby. The American Academy of Pediatrics recommends that babies sleep in their parents' room for the first 6 months to prevent SIDS (American Academy of Pediatrics, 2011).

There are many safe-sleep options. Every family develops its own nighttime variations that work best for them. Here are some choices.

Figure 11-2. *Keeping your baby close at night means less moving around so you can get back to sleep faster.* ©2014 Ameda, Inc. Used with permission.

- Your baby sleeps in a bassinet next to your bed.

- Your baby sleeps in a sidecar bed attached to yours.

- Your baby sleeps in a crib with the side next to your

bed removed and the crib pushed against your bed for easy access.

- Your baby sleeps in a crib elsewhere in your room.

- Your baby sleeps in your bed (using the safe sleep guidelines below) for all or part of the night.

- Your baby (or you and your baby together) sleep on a mattress (or a pallet, a sleeping bag, etc.) on the floor in your room.

Wherever your baby sleeps, you need to know about safe and unsafe sleeping practices. Those listed below are adapted from the guidelines of the Academy of Breastfeeding Medicine (*www.bfmed.org*). The American Academy of Pediatrics also published safe-sleep recommendations (American Academy of Pediatrics, 2011).

If you sleep in a standard American adult bed, products are available, such as guard rails and bolsters, that can prevent falls and make your bed safe for your baby. Or you can put your mattress on the floor away from walls. In Japan, where bedsharing is the norm and many families sleep on futons on the floor, their SIDS rate is among the lowest in the world (McKenna & McDade, 2005). Dawn B. from Georgia, USA, who worked full time in customer service for a manufacturing company, found regular bedsharing the best answer for her and her family.

My baby was 10 weeks old when I returned to work. I truly believe that bedsharing helped me continue breastfeeding while working. I've described having a baby and working as holding down three full-time jobs: the baby, your job, and your household/relationship with your partner. Anything that makes that easier is a plus. Getting sleep at night makes it easier.

Safe Sleeping Practices for any Location

- Put your baby on his back to sleep.

- Use a firm, flat surface, such as a firm mattress on the floor away from walls, or a co-sleeping baby bed (sidecar) or crib that can attach to an adult bed.

- Tuck in any blankets around the mattress to avoid covering your baby's head.

- Dress your baby in a warm sleeper if the room is cold.

- Keep your baby in your room at night for the first six months.

Unsafe sleeping practices

- Your baby should not bedshare with a smoker.

- Don't sleep with your baby on a sofa, couch, recliner, daybed, or waterbed, or with pillows, stuffed toys, or loose bedding near baby.

- Don't bedshare if impaired by alcohol, sedatives, or other drugs.

- Don't sleep in a bed with an adjacent space where your baby could fall or that could trap your baby.

Most parents sleep with their baby some of the time, sometimes unintentionally, so as a precaution, make your bed safe for your baby. Even if you don't plan for you and your baby to fall asleep there, breastfeeding releases hormones that relax you, so it may happen.

Learn to breastfeed lying down. No mother should have to choose between getting her rest and feeding her baby. Breastfeeding lying down allows you to sleep and feed at the same time. Even if this doesn't come easily to you, know that it gets easier with practice.

Practice this at a time you feel awake and alert. Your own best way of breastfeeding lying down may be unique and will depend on your body type. See the images below for some approaches to try.

Nap on your day off. Even if you can't fit in catnaps on work days, getting in a good nap on at least one day off can make all the difference. Kristine R. from Connecticut, USA, a full-time middle-school teacher considered this strategy a lifesaver.

> I went back when my kids were 8.5 and 11 months. They woke several times a night up to about 23 months. I did many things to keep supply high and satisfy my baby's need for closeness (cluster-feed before and after work, nurse a lot on the weekends, nurse at night, bedsharing), but almost every week-end, I got in a good nap on one of the days. That was key for me: catching up on sleep when someone else could be in charge of the baby! I made sure to not over plan for the weekends so I could be sure to catch a nap. That was something I found easy to do because after a busy week of being a working parent, I just wanted to relax and be with my kids anyway. Taking an hour or 2 to myself to nap made me able to give more of myself at night and during the week, which were pretty demanding.

Figure 11-3. *The baby's head rests on the bed and the mother leans back into the pillow. Notice the rolled baby blanket the mother wedged behind her baby leaves her head free to angle back.*

Figure 11-4. *This mother supports her baby's head on her arm.*

Figure 11-5. *One way to breastfeed twins while lying down is with pillows under your arms for support.*

What to Expect as Baby Grows

Although you can expect for your baby's sleep patterns to change as he grows, keep your expectations realistic. On average, breastfed babies wake as much at night to feed at 6 months as they do at 1 month (Kent et al., 2006). Even into their second year, breastfeeding babies and toddlers do not have the same sleep patterns as non-breastfed babies.

But individual differences play a role in babies' sleep too. Differences in mothers' breast storage capacity, for example, mean that some thriving breastfed babies sleep for long stretches at night early on, while others need to breastfeed at night even at 8 months, 10 months, and beyond. Many mothers expect that as their babies grow, they will sleep more and more. However, even the baby who has been sleeping well at night for a while often starts waking again as the discomfort of teething begins. More frequent night waking can also happen as babies begin learning new skills, such as crawling and walking. So if your baby starts sleeping for long periods at night, don't expect this will continue. There are many reasons babies wake at night and want comfort, even when they're not hungry. You may find that as your baby grows, your nighttime solutions change. That's what happened with Kaia and her daughter.

My solution was various forms of co-sleeping. She slept in her swing in our room for months because of severe reflux. I tried bedsharing then but she couldn't because it was too flat. At age 10 months or so, she was more comfortable lying flat so I moved her to our bed. When she started being really mobile in her sleep, I converted her crib into a side-car because of fears she'd roll out of the bed. We did that for a few months until my husband went away for work for a long period. We moved her crib to the corner of our room with the plan being to transition her, but I enjoyed having her back in bed with me, so I just bedshared. She is now 2, nurses only to sleep in our bed, and then is put into her crib in our room asleep. If she wakes during the night and will not go back to sleep, she comes into our bed with us. She woke every two hours until she was over a year old, so I don't know how I would've managed without co-sleeping in its various permutations.

Every family decides how to best handle their babies' night feedings. Be open to trying different strategies at different ages. As Kaia and her family found, both her and her baby's needs and preferences changed as the months passed.

Now that we've covered the basics on how to plan your day (and night) to ensure good milk production, let's address how to know and what to do if your milk production needs a boost.

12

Troubleshooting Milk Production

The single biggest concern mothers have about breast-feeding is whether they're producing enough milk. Often this concern is based on confusion. For that reason, this entire chapter focuses on that topic. We've covered the basics of milk production in Chapter 3 and 11. Let's focus here on how you can tell if your milk production is what it should be and what to do if it isn't.

Baby Takes More Milk Than You Pump

During the many years that I've helped employed breastfeeding mothers, I've often gotten calls that start with, "My baby is taking more milk than I pump." The most important thing to know about this situation is that it doesn't always mean there's a milk-supply issue. There can be other causes completely unrelated to milk production. So before making any changes, first determine what the real issue is. Once you pinpoint it, you can focus your time and energy in the right place. A good place to start is to first compare the amount of milk your baby takes with what's expected.

Compare Your Baby's Milk Intake to What's Expected

Chapter 9 described expected milk intake in more detail, but on average, assume your 1-to-6-month old baby feeding around the clock will drink:

- 7.5 oz. (225 mL) in six hours

- 10 oz. (300 mL) in eight hours

- 15 oz. (450 mL) in 12 hours

As described in Chapter 7, unless bottle-feedings are paced to be more like breastfeeding, babies often take more milk from the bottle than from the breast because of its more consistent flow. This may mean your baby will feed less often than usual while bottle fed.

If Milk Intake Is More Than Expected

These estimated feeding volumes are based on averages, so your baby's intake may be off by a little. But if your baby is taking much more milk than expected, consider one or more of the following possible reasons.

- Bottles are fed at times when your baby could be breastfeeding, such as at drop-off or pick-up or while you are together.

- Your baby is sleeping for stretches longer than 6 hours or so at night so he needs to consume more of his daily 30 oz. while you're at work (see "Calculating Baby's Milk Needs" in Chapter 9).

- Too-fast milk flow from the bottle is causing overfeeding (see Chapter 8 for strategies to prevent this).

- The bottles contain more milk than your baby takes and some milk is being discarded.

- Your baby is being fed more than needed, perhaps as a substitute for focused attention.

Sometimes a simple adjustment in daily routine is all that's needed. Claire's experience is a good example. Claire had just started back to work two weeks before and was frustrated because her 12-week-old baby was taking 20 oz. (600 mL) of pumped milk during her eight-hour work day and she couldn't keep up. Twenty ounces (600 mL) is twice the milk expected (two-thirds of a baby's daily 30 oz./900 mL during one-third of the day). Claire said at work she was "only" pumping 12 oz. (360 mL), which was just a little more than the expected 10 oz. (300 mL). When I asked Claire about her baby's feeding pattern during her work day, here's what she said her baby was taking:

- One 5-oz. (150 mL) bottle of pumped milk when he arrived at daycare.

- Two more 5-oz. (150 mL) bottles during the day.

- A fourth 5-oz. (150 mL) bottle right before she picked him up so that he wouldn't be hungry on the trip home.

After consuming that much milk at daycare, not surprisingly, Claire's baby wasn't very interested in breastfeeding when they got home.

Yet the solution was simple. All Claire needed to do differently was to breastfeed her baby at daycare right before she left him in the morning for work (taking the place of one 5-oz./150 mL bottle) and ask the caregiver to feed just a little milk if needed until she got there to breastfeed before the ride home (taking the place of another 5-oz./150 mL bottle).

This small change in routine made a huge difference in two ways: it added two more feedings at the breast and at the same time cut in half the amount of pumped milk her baby needed at daycare. Instead of taking four 5-oz. (150 mL) bottles at daycare, her baby now only needed two. And the 12 oz. (360 mL) Claire was pumping at work more than covered the 10 oz. (300 mL) her baby was now taking while she was gone. Problem solved!

If Milk Intake Is What's Expected

If your baby's milk intake while you're at work is in the range you expect, but what you're pumping does not meet your baby's need, that's an entirely different issue. Read on.

Compare Your Pump Yield to What's Expected

Breastfed babies take on average 3 to 4 oz. (90-120 mL) per feeding. When you replace a missed feeding by pumping at work, expect to pump a full feeding. So if your pumping sessions yield 3 to 4 oz. (90-120 mL), consider this average.

If Pump Yield Is What's Expected

If your pump yield is in this expected range, this means the issue with your baby's milk intake is due to factors unrelated to your milk production. See the previous section for possibilities.

If Pump Yield Is Less Than Expected

If your pump yield is less than average, it's time to consider the following issues:

- Your pump isn't working properly.

- Your pump isn't working effectively for you.

- Your milk supply is less than what's needed.

If you think the problem might be with your pump function, contact the manufacturer, who can troubleshoot it with you. This is well worth a phone call, because if your pump is within its warranty period, they may even send you replacement parts or a whole new pump.

If the pump's effectiveness for you may be the issue, review the section "Realistic Pumping Expectations" in Chapter 5 for pumping strategies and try any that are new *"We used to think the breast pump should do all of the milk-removal work, but we know now that using your hands can make a big difference."* to you. Be sure to try the hands-on pumping techniques, the tips to trigger more milk releases, and the other tips for improving milk yields. We used to think the breast pump should do all of the milk-removal work, but we know now that using your hands can make a big difference. Emotional stress can block milk releases or reduce the number of milk releases per pump session, so if your workplace is stressful, you may temporarily pump less milk. The techniques in Chapter 5 can help you get your milk yields back on track by stimulating more milk releases. Between now and then, see the later section "Extra Pump Sessions."

As also mentioned in Chapter 5, in a small percentage of mothers, breast pumps—even good ones—do not work effectively. This might apply to you if your exclusively breast-fed baby is gaining weight normally and you've never (not once) gotten the expected milk yield with a pump. In this case, try hand expression (see the Appendix B for instructions). If you have previously pumped the expected milk volumes, you know this isn't the problem.

If the issue seems to be with your milk supply, first review in Chapter 11 the sections, "The Magic Number" and "Impact of Daily Routines." Then read the next section.

Extra Pump Sessions

Some employed mothers pump nearly, but not quite all the milk their babies take while they're at work. Maybe they can't fit in enough pump sessions during their work day or maybe their pump just doesn't drain them as effectively and consistently as their baby. If you find yourself in this situation and your goal is to provide your milk only for your baby, one option is to do some extra pump sessions to make up for your shortfall.

Pump at Home

How can you make this work? Here are some possibilities:

- When you get up for the day, pump either one or both breasts before your baby nurses. For some, this works really well. For others, not so much.

- If your baby goes to bed for the night before you, do an extra pump session right before you go to sleep.

- Pump once if you wake up in the middle of the night. Many mothers find that due to the higher prolactin (a milk-enhancing hormone) levels at night, they get the most milk then.

- Pump 30 to 60 minutes after some feedings in the evening or on your days off. That timing will usually give you more milk to store than pumping right after breastfeeding, but it should not affect the milk that's available to your baby at the next feeding.

Figure 12-1. *Whether pumping at home or at work, breast compression and massage can increase milk yields.* ©2014 Ameda, Inc. Used with permission.

Pump in the Car

No book for employed mothers would be complete without a mention of pumping during your commute to or from work. Pumping and driving is not recommended for safety reasons. (Like phoning or texting while driving, the distraction of pumping can increase your risk of accidents.) Even so, some mothers do this, presumably hands free so they can keep both hands on the wheel.

But perhaps you are not driving. Maybe your partner is driving or someone else whom you don't mind pumping alongside. In this case, you may take advantage of this time to fit in another pump session.

Other Pump Options

Some mothers find that if they pump first thing upon arriving at work (rather than waiting for a couple of hours) that enough time has passed that they get a good amount of milk. Experiment to see if that works for you.

How to Boost Milk Supply

In some situations, boosting your milk supply is not a good idea. For example, if your baby is younger than 6 months, your pump yields are average, your baby is receiving your milk exclusively, and is gaining weight well, boosting milk production may not be wise. In this case "more" is not necessarily "better." Boosting your supply too high has drawbacks. As described in Chapter 3, mothers with oversupply are at greater risk of leaking milk, regular breast discomfort, and developing mastitis (a painful breast condition also described in Chapter 3).

Another situation in which boosting milk production might not be necessary is if your baby is older than 6 months and is eating solid foods. In this case, gradually slowing milk production is normal as your baby's need for milk decreases. If you are pumping enough milk to meet your baby's needs, you don't need to increase your milk production.

When *do* you want to boost supply? You definitely want to consider it if your baby's weight gain has slowed on your milk alone or you are running out of milk to leave while you're at work. In these situations, it's definitely time to act.

Sooner Rather Than Later

If you need to boost milk production, don't wait to take steps to increase it. If you have a low supply and wait longer than three-to-four weeks, it becomes harder to boost it. It most definitely can be done. It just requires much more time and effort. That's why if you want to raise your production, do it soon.

Strategies to Boost Supply

Some mothers think that either they will be gifted with abundant milk or they won't, and they have nothing to say about it. Hopefully, you know by now that in most cases, milk production is under your control. Here's what you need to do to give your milk supply a boost.

More Milk Removals

This is the most important part of boosting supply. The herbs and medications mentioned next will not help you unless you are also doing this. For most women, between 8 and 12 milk removals per day will cause a gradual increase in milk production. (Being at your magic number will just keep production steady.) The exact number needed to boost production for you will depend on your storage capacity and your individual body's response to breast stimulation. Table 12-1 estimates, based on breast storage capacity, how many milk removals per day may be enough to boost supply. This information comes from observation and hopefully will serve as a starting point for research on it.

There are three ways to increase daily milk removals: breastfeed more, pump more, and do both. The choice is yours. For most women, more breastfeeding requires far less time and effort than more pumping. (There's nothing to clean and it accomplishes feeding and stimulation at the same time.) But it is entirely your decision. You should do whichever combination of these you prefer and whichever makes most sense in your situation. For some mothers, for example, it may make sense to take a few days off work, stay in bed with drinks and snacks handy, and have a "baby-moon," where they nurse like crazy to boost their supply. But taking time off work is not possible for everyone. If this is you, keep reading for other options.

	Largest Capacity	Large Capacity	Medium Capacity	Small Capacity	Smallest Capacity
To Boost Supply	4-5	6-8	8-10	10-11	≥12
To maintain Supply	3-4	5	6	7	8
To Slow Supply	2	3	4-5	6	7

Table 12-1. *Estimated effect of milk removals per day on milk production*

If you're pumping, know that some women get better results with a rental-grade pump. If you haven't been doing it before, this is the time to start using hands-on pumping techniques to drain your breasts more fully each time. (Drained breasts make milk faster.) Hands-on pumping was found to boost milk production by 48% in women pumping for their premature babies in the special-care nursery. It is described in detail in the section, "Factors That Affect Milk Yield" in Chapter 5, along with other strategies for improving pumping milk yields.

When to pump. The most important point to keep in mind is that you don't have to either feed or pump at regular intervals in order to send your body the signal to make more milk. At home, for example, you can pump every hour while your baby naps and it will have the same effect on increasing milk production as pumping after longer time intervals.

If you're pumping to boost production, decide which of these makes sense for you:

- Pump more times at work.

- Pump at home, either right after breastfeeding or after waiting 30 to 60 minutes.

The drawback of pumping right after breastfeeding is that you'll get less milk than if you wait 30 to 60 minutes. Even so, pumping right after breastfeeding will still help stimulate milk production. (Drained breasts make milk faster.) Choose those strategies you're more likely to actually do. A plan is only as good as its follow-through.

You may find pumping easier to do at some times of the day than others. Give these approaches a try and see how you feel about them:

- Pump often when your partner or a helper is around to care for your baby. (No mother should have to pump while her baby is fussy and needs attention.)

- Pump in the middle of the night.

Nighttime pumps usually yield more milk, which can be encouraging. Take a cold, hard look at your 24-hour day and try pumping at different times. Then stick with whatever works best for you.

Power pumping. This strategy has never been studied, and it means different things to different people. To some, power pumping means having their pump set up and ready to go in an area of their home that they pass often and sitting down to pump for at least 5 to 10 minutes whenever they pass it (West & Marasco, 2009). (To simplify this, some suggest leaving the same pump parts attached and reusing them for whatever length of time your milk is safe at room temperature before washing.) For others, it means spending an hour pumping, 10 minutes on and 10 minutes off (maybe while they're watching a movie or television show). Anything that increases the number of milk removals is bound to help. We just don't know how power pumping (in either of its forms) compares to other strategies.

Balancing pumping with the rest of your life. It's never a good idea to get into a routine that feels overwhelming. Whatever approach you choose, it needs to be one that you can do for a time and not feel like you're going crazy. It's also fine to take a break from the extra pumping for a while and come back to it later. Babies sometimes have "frequency days" (sometimes called "growth spurts"), when they go into nursing frenzies. You can do the same with pumping. Pumping intensively for a short time (maybe every hour during your waking hours over the weekend) is better for your milk production than not doing it at all.

Herbs and Medications

When combined with more milk removals, in some cases taking certain herbs and medications can help boost supply. The herb fenugreek has a long history of use to increase milk production in Egypt and India. The U.S. Food and Drug Administration has given it a rating of generally recognized as safe (GRAS). But if you have blood-sugar or thyroid issues, or are taking prescription or over-the-counter medications, discuss it with your health care provider before you take it. The dose to boost milk production is three to four capsules (of at least 500 mg each, three times per day (9 to 12 total). You can buy fenugreek at health food stores. It is also available online in capsules and in liquid tincture form. For more information on other herbs thought to increase milk, such as alfalfa, blessed thistle, nettle, goat's rue, and shatavari, see: *http://www.lowmilksupply.org/increasingmilk-galactagogues.shtml.*

Two prescription medications are found to increase milk production in some women: metoclopramide and domperidone. Both drugs are normally prescribed for stomach problems. Domperidone is currently under an FDA ban in the U.S., but is available in other countries. Since depression can be a side effect of metoclopramide, you may want to avoid it if you have a history of depression (Hale, 2012). There is also a rare side effect that happens most often when metoclopramide is taken longer than one month called tardive dyskenisia, or involuntary grimacing, which can be permanent. Both of these side effects make metoclopramide a less-than-optimal choice, but it can be helpful in some circumstances.

Foods and Drinks

Are there foods and drinks that increase milk production? Many online forums recommend eating oatmeal and lactation cookies, or drinking beer (they say non-alcoholic beer works, too). The fact is, we don't really know whether or not these foods and drinks affect milk production. There's certainly nothing harmful in consuming foods that are believed to be milk-enhancing. But the most important area of focus should be increasing the number of daily milk removals.

For more on possible causes and treatments for low milk production, see the book, *The Breastfeeding Mothers' Guide to Making More Milk*, by Diana West and Lisa Marasco.

Your Freezer Stash and Other Supplements

Having a large reserve of frozen milk can give a mother a real feeling of security, but how you use what's in your freezer can work for you or against you. Here are some ways your freezer stash can work for you.

- You have an off-day at work and miss a pump or two and you don't have enough refrigerated milk for the next day.

- You forget to take your pumped milk out of your cooler compartment after work on Friday and it is spoiled by the time you find it on Sunday night.

- You spill all the milk you just pumped.

In other words, using the milk in your freezer is a great choice when the unexpected happens. Now let's look at how using your freezer stash can work against you.

A Consistent Shortfall

Times you should be cautious about using your frozen milk reserve is when it becomes your regular go-to place. For example, if every day for a week straight you pump 3 oz. (90 mL), less than what your baby needs for the next day, this is a red flag that something needs adjusting. You can certainly use your frozen milk, but you also need to look into why this is happening and try to change it. Most likely your shortfall is a sign you've slipped below your magic number (see Chapter 11).

A giant freezer stash may give you a false sense of security. Think about it. If you give your baby 3 oz. (90 mL) of frozen milk every single day, before long your freezer stash will be gone and you will still be short of milk. If your goal is to exclusively breastfeed and your baby is consistently taking any amount of frozen milk or formula every day, don't be complacent. See this as a sign that it's time to get to the root of your milk-production issue, and boost it to where it needs to be. (See the previous section for strategies.) Think long term. Don't ignore regular shortfalls.

Weaning Off Supplements

If you've decided to take action, the next question becomes: What do you do? You obviously need to feed your baby. Where do you start?

Make Sure All Bottle Feeds Are Paced

If you haven't yet given your caregiver a copy of Appendix A: For the Caregiver of a Breastfed Baby, now's the time. This handout (see also Chapter 8) describes how to pace bottle feeds, which in some cases, cuts feeding volumes by as much as half. Pacing bottle feeds changes feeding dynamics to be more like breastfeeding.

On average, when fed at the breast, babies are satisfied with less milk than when fed by bottle in the traditional way (baby leaning back, bottle nearly vertical). If your baby takes less milk by bottle, she will be a more active feeder at the breast, stimulating more milk production. Drained breasts make milk faster.

Reduce Gradually the Milk in the Bottle

To wean a baby off of the extra supplement, think about how to gradually shift her milk intake to take less from the bottle and more from you. Obviously, you don't want your baby to feel hungry and deprived, so it's important to watch and respond to your baby's cues.

One way is to slightly reduce the amount of milk your baby gets while you're at work. If your baby usually takes 5 oz. (150 mL) from the bottle at daycare, for example, instead leave 4.5 oz. (135 mL) bottles. Then plan to add in an extra breastfeed while you're together. Remember, what matters most to a baby is not how much milk she gets per feeding, but how much milk she gets in 24 hours. It may be possible to reduce the amount of milk your baby takes while you're at work by breastfeeding more at home (see next section).

Keep in mind that breastfed babies take on average 3 to 4 oz. (90 to 120 mL) per feeding. If you can adjust how your baby is bottle fed while you're apart to mimic that, it may make her a more active nurser when you're together and reduce the amount of milk she needs while you're apart.

If you are supplementing your baby with bottles at home after breastfeeding, offer each breast several times before supplementing (see next section). Plan to gradually reduce the amount of milk in the bottle over time. For example, if you usually give your baby 2 oz. (60 mL) after breast-feeding, instead give 1.5 oz. (45 mL). If baby still seems hungry, put her back to the breast. Remember from Chapter 7, your breasts are never empty. She can easily get another half ounce (15 mL) from you directly if she just keeps breastfeeding. Move your baby back and forth from breast to breast until she seems done. This will also boost your milk production. (Drained breasts make milk faster.)

Each time you reduce the amount of supplement and breastfeed more, give your body at least two to three days to boost milk production. Then, if appropriate, reduce the supplement after each breastfeeding by another half ounce (15 mL). Continue until you are weaned from the supplement.

Breastfeed More

Review the section "The Impact of Daily Routines" in Chapter 11 for a refresher on how more breastfeeding can reduce the amount of milk your baby needs from the bottle. Here are two simple strategies that can make a big difference.

Offer each breast at least twice. Chapter 3 explained that on average breastfed babies take about two thirds of the milk in the breast, leaving one third. If your baby still seems hungry after taking both breasts, go back to the first breast and start over. Chapter 7 explained that your breasts are never empty. There's always a little more. By encouraging your baby to take more, you also make milk faster. Another strategy that may help while you do this is called "breast compression." See Canadian pediatrician Jack Newman's website for instructions: *http://www.breastfeedinginc. ca/content.php?pagename=doc-BC*

Offer to breastfeed more often. Maybe you've already done this, but to be on the safe side, review the section "Ways to Fit in More Breastfeeding" in Chapter 11.

Even if you're not happy with your milk production now, this is something you can change. Hopefully, you now have some ideas for how to move closer to your goal.

Now let's end our adventures in working and breast-feeding by discussing the changes you can expect as your baby grows and ways to think about weaning.

13

Changes as Your Baby Grows

You may have turned to this chapter because you want to think ahead. Or if your maternity leave is six months or longer, you may be wondering what you need to know about returning to work when your baby is older than 6 months. This chapter covers some of the many ways babies and breastfeeding change over the months: the impact of solid foods, teething, and distractibility. It also focuses on you and your goals. Some women breastfeed the length of time they first envisioned. Some decide to breastfeed longer. Some choose—or are forced by circumstances—to fall short of their original target. Because every woman who starts breastfeeding eventually weans, this chapter includes strategies for making weaning comfortable and positive, as well as ways to make peace with any changes in plan. It also includes mothers' perspective on their experience after they've had time to look back and reflect.

From 6 to 12 Months and Beyond

Babies change so quickly! The tiny newborn who had trouble lifting her head is soon sitting, crawling, pulling up, and walking. The first year is a time of miraculous growth and development. Breastfeeding also changes with your baby. This section covers some of what you can expect as the months pass.

Feeding Patterns

Although feeding patterns don't usually change much during a baby's first six months, don't be surprised during the second six months, if you notice some of the following:

- Your baby cues to breastfeed less often.

- Your baby breastfeeds for a shorter time.

- Your baby is easily distracted during many feedings.

At this stage, all of these behaviors are part of normal growth and change.

Driven to Distraction

Beginning at around 3 months, most babies become distracted during feedings. Whether the trigger is someone talking or even the cat walking by, babies this age will sometimes pull off, or worse, turn their head to look without pulling off. Ouch! As babies grow, distractibility increases, sometimes to the point that you wonder if your baby is ready to wean. But this is a normal part of breastfeeding the older baby. Keep in mind that babies need mother's milk (or a substitute like formula) during their entire first year. Babies younger than 1 year are not yet physically ready to wean, even if they seem distracted much of the time.

Because most babies become speed feeders at this stage, many mothers wonder if your baby is getting enough milk. The same baby who, as a newborn, breastfed 30 to 40 minutes at a session may now pop off or lose interest after just 5 minutes. Keep in mind that over time, babies get milk from the breast much faster. At this age, your baby likely takes more milk in 5 minutes than she did during those long, leisurely nursings during her early weeks. As always, the bottom line is your baby's weight gain and growth. A healthy weight gain tells you that she's getting what she needs, despite short feedings.

As mentioned in the Chapter 11 section on sleep, during this time, many babies (some of whom may have slept well during the early months) are often wakeful at night and want to breastfeed. This is how many distractible babies make up for lost time. As babies learn new skills, such as crawling, pulling up, and walking, they become so fixated on practicing these new skills that they often attempt them while in a light sleep, awakening themselves at night. The discomfort of teething is another reason why many older babies wake and want to nurse. Breastfeeding has always been an all-purpose mothering tool. It is fine to nurse for comfort as well as for milk. In fact, as babies grow, it's almost impossible to separate the two! For the older baby, the comfort of breastfeeding becomes as important to her as the milk.

Solid Foods and Milk Production

As mentioned before, when your baby takes more solid foods, she needs less milk (Islam, Peerson, Ahmed, Dewey, & Brown, 2006). But there is such a large variation in how quickly babies take to solid foods that it's hard to predict exactly how this will play out over your baby's second six months. Keep in mind that during this time, your milk (or infant formula) should still be your baby's main food. At this stage, think of solids as a supplement to the milk. Here's what the World Health Organization has to say:

> Breast milk is an important source of energy and nutrients in children aged 6 to 23 months. It can provide half or more of a child's energy needs between the ages of 6 and 12 months, and one third of energy needs between 12 and 24 months. Breast milk is also a critical source of energy and nutrients during illness... (WHO, 2010).

How much milk can you expect to produce as your baby grows? Among 15-month-old breastfeeding babies, scientists in Australia measured milk intake at between 3 and 10 oz. (95 to 315 mL) per day (Kent, Mitoulas, Cox, Owens, & Hartmann, 1999; Neville et al., 1991). But of course milk intake depends on how much your baby breastfeeds. (Drained breasts still make milk faster.) Research in countries where breastfeeding older babies is the norm, found that at 30 months mothers' produced, on average, 10 oz. (300 mL) per day (Hennart, Delogne-Desnoeck, Vis, & Robyn, 1981). In other words, if your baby nurses often, your milk may be a large part of her diet, even after 2 years.

Figure 13-1. *Even if your baby eats lots of solid foods, your milk is still an important part of her diet.*

Teething and Biting

Around the age when babies' teeth erupt (on average, about 7 months), many mothers worry their baby might bite. Some mothers are even cautioned to wean by that age as a precaution. But many babies never bite, and those who bite once usually never bite again. However, if biting is an issue for you, there are ways to discourage it.

Use Cold Before Breastfeeding

If your teething baby is bearing down or biting during breastfeeding, before latching, try numbing her gums by giving her something cold to chew on, such as a cold, wet washcloth or a refrigerated teething toy. If baby has started solid foods, another option is to first give her frozen peas or blueberries to eat. Applying cold to her sore gums may relieve pain and prevent problems.

Other Strategies to Discourage Biting

One of the most important (and sometimes most diffi-cult) things to do to discourage biting is to try to stay calm, break the suction, and take your baby off. Pulling your baby off the breast with her teeth clamped down can cause more damage than the bite itself. These strategies may help dis-courage a persistent biter.

- **Stop the feeding**. Remove the temptation for your baby to make you jump.

- **Offer something else to bite on,** such as a teething ring or toy.

- **Set your baby quickly on the floor,** so biting brings negative consequences. After a few seconds of distress, comfort her.

- **Keep a finger near your baby's mouth,** ready to break the suction if she turns away and pulls on your nipple. If you respond consistently, your baby will learn quickly that turning away means losing the nipple.

- **Make sure your baby latches deeply,** which lessens the odds of biting.

Here are more tried-and-true strategies.

- **Give your baby your complete attention during breastfeeding.** Eye contact, stroking, and talking decrease the odds that she will bite for attention.

- **Learn to recognize the signs** that your baby is losing interest in breastfeeding, when most biting occurs.

- **Avoid pressuring a disinterested baby to breastfeed.** Try again later.

- **Remove a sleeping baby** by breaking the suction.

- **Note behaviors that lead to biting.** Some babies bite when teased or when you raise your voice.

- **Praise your baby when she doesn't bite**. Say, "good baby" when she is gentle. Give smiles, hugs, and kisses.

Ways to Reduce Discomfort

While experimenting with strategies to discourage bearing down or biting, use the following to reduce any pain.

- **Take ibuprofen** or another analgesia that your health care provider recommends.

- **Offer your less-sore breast first**, and then switch to the other after your milk is flowing.

- **Vary feeding positions** so one area is not consistently hurt.

- **Use ultrapurified lanolin or hydrogel pads** after feeding to lessen pain.

Babies don't understand that biting causes pain. Breastfeeding teaches your baby to associate you with feelings of security, comfort, and relief from hunger. When these positive associations are disrupted by biting, she should learn quickly not to do it again.

Breastfeeding the Older Baby and Toddler

Professional health groups, such as the American Academy of Pediatrics and the World Health Organization recommend breastfeeding for at least 1 to 2 years (AAP, 2012;

WHO, 2010). Why? Because the science tells us that the lifelong health of mother and child are measurably worse when breastfeeding ends earlier. If you're undecided about how long to breastfeed, a summary of what you and your baby stand to gain might help put this in perspective.

What's in It for You?

Why is continued breastfeeding a plus for you? For one, you get more and better rest. Science tells us that while a mother breastfeeds, she sleeps longer and deeper and her metabolism is more efficient than after weaning (Kendall-Tackett, Cong, & Hale, 2011; Stuebe & Rich-Edwards, 2009). Fatigue is a normal part of early motherhood. But this is true no matter how a baby is fed and whether or not a mother is employed.

Continued breastfeeding is also better for your long-term health. The longer and more exclusively you breastfeed and the more months total you breastfeed during your lifetime, the better. Even decades after your baby weans, cutting breastfeeding short increases your risk of developing breast and ovarian cancers, rheumatoid arthritis, type 2 diabetes, metabolic syndrome, and heart disease, the number one killer of women (Stuebe & Schwarz, 2010).

Of course, there's far more to breastfeeding than your rest or your health. Becca A. from Tennessee, USA wrote about the emotional reasons she chose to keep breastfeeding:

Nursing sessions with your baby before work, after work, at bedtimes, and during the night were so special to me. It was our time to reconnect and catch up on the day. I wouldn't trade them for anything.

Amy L., a full-time public-health nurse from Ontario, Canada described another reason she was glad she was breastfeeding after a year:

After a one-year maternity leave, I went back to my full-time work with both of my children and continued to breastfeed at home. When my children went to daycare, they sometimes got sick. I was so thankful I was breastfeeding because when ill, they would not eat and drink much, but they would always nurse! I did not have to worry about them getting enough nutrients to sustain them and get well. I also loved the time we shared before and after work; it is not often that you get to come home and relax with a snuggle before you get on with your evening.

What Your Baby Gains

Ignore the naysayers who tell you that mother's milk has no value to your baby after a specific age. As long as your baby breastfeeds, she receives antibodies from your milk that protect her from illness. In studies on older children, even up to age 3 years, weaned children were sicker and sick more often than their breastfeeding counterparts

(Molbak et al., 1994). The living antibodies in mother's milk work their magic for as long as your child nurses.

Weaning before one year increases your baby's risk of coming down with colds, ear infections, diarrhea, meningitis, bronchitis, pneumonia, and other illnesses. But the effects of breastfeeding on your baby's health extend far beyond babyhood. Weaning before age 1 also increases her risk later in life of long-term health problems, such as obesity, allergies, diabetes, celiac disease, and inflammatory bowel diseases (AAP, 2012).

When it comes to nutrition, I've always found it curious that anyone would think that the milk of another animal (i.e., dairy) could be more nutritious for our babies than our own milk. It defies logic! No matter what your baby's age is, your milk is packed with nutrients uniquely designed to enhance her growth and development. Scientists estimate that breastfed babies 1 to 2 years old who get average amounts of mother's milk receive 35% to 40% of their energy intake from it (Dewey & Brown, 2003). Human milk is an important source of fatty acids and other key nutrients, such as vitamin A, calcium, and riboflavin (PAHO/WHO., 2001).

But there's much more to this picture than just your baby's health and nutrition. As mentioned before, as your baby matures, the comfort and closeness of breastfeeding become even more important to her than the milk. Nursing helps older babies and toddlers cope with the hurts and the stresses that are a natural part of growing up. And the closer they feel to you, the greater your influence on them and their values as they grow. The closeness of nursing can help smooth over many challenges of the early years.

Crystal N., a full-time public health nurse in Manitoba, Canada, enjoys her baby's reaction when she gets home from work in the evening.

> I went back to work four months ago when the youngest of my three girls was 12 months old. My youngest at that point was still breastfeeding on demand, and demanding she was! :) She loves to breastfeed! She would wait for me to get home. I would sit her on my bed while I changed out of my work clothes. When I would take off my shirt she would start to pant, and wave her arms around. Sometimes, when I would put my home shirt on, she would cry until I picked her up, carried her to the couch, and sat and nursed her. It was my favorite part of the day. Just to sit and cuddle her.

Phasing Out Pumping

No matter how devoted you are to breastfeeding, every mother eventually stops pumping at work. Most often, this happens at or near 1 year, because at that age, your baby can start drinking milk from the dairy case. If your family doesn't drink cow's milk, water is an option, as well as other milks and liquids (see Chapter 8). Some mothers decide to continue pumping at work after 12 months. Sometimes it's because their babies are sensitive or allergic, or they just prefer their babies to drink their milk. At some point, though, every mother stops pumping.

Whenever you decide to phase out pumping, to reduce the risk of discomfort and breast problems, make any changes gradually. For example, if you've been pumping three times during your workday, cut down to two times and give your body at least three to four days for your milk production to adjust downwards. Then cut back to one pump at work and give your body three to four days to adjust before you stop pumping altogether.

If you ever feel uncomfortably full during that time, pump just to comfort. This means pumping long enough to make your breasts comfortable, but no longer. Pumping to comfort will not prolong the process. It will simply make you more comfortable and reduce your risk of breast problems.

Rethinking Your Goals

Many mothers find the reality of parenting much different than they imagined. In this case, as well as when circumstances change, it may make sense for you to reevaluate the breastfeeding goals you set before your baby was born.

Breastfeeding Longer

When you began breastfeeding, what was your personal goal? Six weeks? Three months? Six months? One year?

Two years? Whatever it was, when you get there, you may wonder if it is really the right time to wean.

Can you breastfeed too long?

Many women wonder if it is harmful for them or their baby to breastfeed longer than a specific age. It may help to know that health associations, such as the American Academy of Pediatrics and the World Health Organization, set no upper age limit on breastfeeding. Why? First, from a health standpoint, the longer you breastfeed, the better for both you and your baby. Second, even if you never take steps to wean, they know your baby will eventually outgrow breastfeeding on her own.

Figure 13-2. *Even if others disapprove of nursing past a certain age, experts agree that in terms of your and your baby's health, the longer you breastfeed, the better.*

Some mothers wean before they feel ready because others convince them that they are being "selfish" or harming their child by breastfeeding past a certain age. But what our culture considers normal is at the very

324

early end of the broader human experience. Knowing this can give you more freedom to make your own decisions rather than being swayed by others.

When Do Others Wean?

At what age do children outgrow breastfeeding? That varies by time and place. When human cultures are viewed as a whole, the average age of weaning is between 2 and 4 years, with some breastfeeding for as long as 5 to 7 years. History tells us that breastfeeding for years was a common practice in most times and places, including in the colonial United States. Interestingly, most religions' holy books address the age of weaning. The Quran recommends breastfeeding for at least two years, the Torah three years, and Hindu Ayurvedic texts recommend mother's milk only for the first year with solids gradually replacing it during the second year. Does this mean you should breastfeed this long? Not necessarily. But if you decide to breastfeed longer than most people you know, you can rest assured that this is not harmful to either you or your child.

Giving Formula or Weaning Earlier

Sometimes rather than breastfeeding longer, a mother's best intentions to keep breastfeeding is short-circuited by a specific situation. Other times, she decides the time is right earlier than her original target. If you find it necessary to use formula or consider weaning before you had planned, this is the section for you.

It Doesn't Have to Be All or Nothing

As mentioned in previous chapters, breastfeeding doesn't have to be all or nothing. Some women think that giving any formula means it is pointless to continue breastfeeding. But that's just not true. There is value to both you and your baby in any amount of breastfeeding.

If health is your main reason for breastfeeding, know that partial breastfeeding is better for your baby than stopping entirely. As one example, babies who are not breastfed have twice the ear infections of babies exclusively breastfed. Mixed-fed babies are in the middle (AAP, 2012).

If your main motivation for breastfeeding is for greater closeness, this does not change, even if your baby also receives formula.

Making Peace with Your Experience

If you've given formula or weaned earlier than planned, it may help to hear how others coped with this. It's been more than 10 years, but Jennifer S. from Pennsylvania, USA still thinks about returning to work full- time as the international sales coordinator for a giftware company when her oldest son was 11 weeks old.

When he was about 6 months old, my boss asked me to travel by plane to a sales conference, for which I would be away from my baby for a little over 48 hours. It was the first time my employer asked me to travel, and I felt I had to say yes. My boss didn't show any sympathy towards my breastfeeding needs and I was too afraid to ask. I didn't have any lactation resources, so I tried to use common sense to make the best of my trip.

I had a little pumped milk in the freezer that my husband used to feed the baby while I was gone. Unfortunately, he ran out before I returned and had to go buy formula. That was the first time my baby was given formula. It made me sad because I had worked so hard to avoid giving him formula up until this point.

Although I pumped while I was at the conference, I couldn't get away from meetings often enough. I also had no idea I could ship the milk home, so I dumped it down the drain. I was very sad about that! I was engorged and once I returned home, my milk supply decreased. I tried taking the herb fenugreek to increase it, but it only helped a little. After my return home, my babysitter occasionally had to use formula because I couldn't keep up with my baby's demands. I weaned him at about 9 to 10 months of age.

In my mind, I have always regarded the conference travel as the "difference maker" in the need to use formula and the start of the weaning process. My way of making peace with my experience was to cut myself some slack because I wasn't well informed enough at the time to know my options and to promise myself that I would speak up if a similar situation arose. It was also one reason I later became a postpartum doula and breastfeeding support counselor!

Joy S. from Kentucky, USA, a project manager assistant at a general contracting company, returned to work full-time when her baby was 2 months old:

When my son was 3 months old, he had a growth spurt and I needed to supplement one or two bottles of formula every couple of days. Even with all my pumping, I wasn't keeping up. I felt very discouraged. How bad of a mom am I? The one thing I could provide for him and I was failing. Not only was I away from him all day, I was spending all my free time hooked up to this cold, un-emotional machine and still not able to give him the most important thing he needed.

I realized at one point in the midst of it that I couldn't do it all, and that was okay. I couldn't fit in more pump sessions. I finally just told myself that if we had to supplement a few times, then that was fine. The important thing was a healthy baby. It didn't make me any less of a mom. It didn't diminish the fact that he was still getting a majority of breast milk. He was a growing, healthy, baby boy, so why did I let it stress me out? I was determined to make it to at least 1 year of breastfeeding, and I felt this was interfering with my perfect plan. Why? He was still getting breast milk as much as possible.

It seemed like as soon as I let go of trying to have a perfect plan of exclusively breastfeeding his growth spurt slowed down, and all of a sudden I had enough to replace my freezer stash and add to it. No more supplementing and no more feeling like I had failed. I was also able to slowly cut out the midnight pump session I'd been doing and get more sleep! Going through that helped me be more determined than ever to make it to a year of breastfeeding. But it also helped me to relax, let go, and not stress any more about it. If we survived that, we could survive anything! We have had more growth spurts and times of cutting it close on bottles for the day. But we haven't had to supplement anymore and I am three weeks shy of making it a year and we are still going strong!

In Chapter 10, Joy mentioned that joining a local breast-feeding support group did wonders to raise her spirits. Spending time with other mothers—either in person or online—who have been there, done that can help you feel less alone and relieve stress when you encounter challenges. It can also help you see the positive in your experience. Sometimes just being with someone who understands what you're going through can make all the difference. See the

Resources section for mother-to-mother support options in your area and online.

Weaning Goals and Strategies

Despite what you may have heard, weaning does not have to be a time of pain and deprivation. With these strategies, you can make your weaning as gentle and loving as the way breastfeeding began. The key is to wean gradually. By going slow, you can prevent breast pain and problems. A gradual weaning also gives you time to make sure your baby tolerates well whatever substitutes for your milk you give her. Your baby's age will influence your approach.

Weaning Before 1 Year

The main strategy for weaning a baby younger than about 12 months is to substitute for one feeding at a time a bottle or cup of formula for your milk. Here's how to do a gradual, comfortable weaning.

- First, note the times each day you usually breastfeed.

- Pick one daily breastfeeding or pumping (reserve the first morning feeding for last) and substitute infant formula by bottle or cup at that feeding.

- Allow at least three to four days for your milk supply to slow comfortably before dropping another breastfeeding or pumping.

With this approach, it takes about two to three weeks to go from exclusive breastfeeding to fully weaned.

While you wean, your breasts may sometimes feel full. If so, whenever needed, pump just enough milk to ease your breast fullness and no more. Pumping to comfort will not stimulate more milk. It simply allows your milk supply to reduce gradually enough to prevent breast pain and problems. When in doubt, pump to comfort. Pay attention to your body's cues.

Weaning After 1 Year

The child older than about 12 months usually has strong preferences about all aspects of daily life. But with planning, weaning doesn't have to be an unhappy time. If your child breastfeeds often, allow several weeks to wean fully. As with the weaning of a younger baby, when you drop a breastfeeding, give your body three to four days for your milk supply to slow before dropping the next.

As you wean, respect your baby's preferences. Think about foods, drinks, and activities she might consider better than breastfeeding, and offer them as much as possible. If certain nursings are more important to her, let her to give them up last. Use only those strategies among the following that work well with your child.

- **Don't offer, don't refuse.** Breastfeed when your child asks, and don't offer when she doesn't ask.

331

When used with other strategies, this can speed the process.

- **Make sure your child gets enough to eat and drink**. Children often ask to breastfeed when they're hungry or thirsty. Eliminate this reason with regular meals, snacks, and drinks.

- **Plan interesting activities**. Your child may not even think of breastfeeding if you offer age-appropriate, fun alternatives that keep her happily busy.

- **Change your routine**. Think about when and where your child asks to breastfeed. Then consider changes in routine that will remind her less of nursing.

- **Get your partner involved**. Sleep-related nursings can be the trickiest to eliminate without a fuss, such as going to sleep, while half asleep, or after waking up. When you want to drop the first morning breastfeeding, ask your partner to get your child up for the day and give her breakfast. Your partner can also create new bedtime routines and help her get back to sleep when she wakes, as well as plan daytime outings.

- **Before your child asks, offer substitutes and distractions**. Once she's asked to nurse, offering a substitute may upset her. Try offering a snack before a usual nursing and take her to a favorite place as a distraction.

- **Postpone breastfeeding.** This can work for a child who nurses irregularly and is old enough to accept waiting (age 2 or 3). If postponing leaves your child feeling frustrated, other strategies will be better.

- **Shorten the time spent breastfeeding.** This is most effective with children older than 2 years. Some mothers make learning to use the clock a way to help toddlers know when their time is up.

- **Bargain.** An older child close to outgrowing breast-feeding may give it up earlier by agreement. Under 3 years, most do not understand what a promise means.

- **Be flexible.** When unusual situations arise, avoid sticking rigidly to your plan. If your child is ill, you can go back to weaning when she's feeling better.

Keep in mind that even at the same age, some children will be more ready to wean than others. If your child becomes upset, this may mean that weaning is going too fast or that different strategies would be better. Listen to your own inner voice and be sensitive to your child's cues.

Hindsight is 20/20

If you're still unsure about some of your options, this would be a good time to get in touch with the online and in-person breastfeeding support organizations listed in the Resources Section. There is value in sharing perspectives with other mothers. In fact, a fitting way to end to this book is in a mother's own words. Best of luck with your adventures in working and breastfeeding!

Just before the birth of her second child, Lauren J., a full-time social worker from New York, USA found herself at the perfect time to look back and reflect on her experience.

> My son was only 8 weeks old when I had to return to my full-time job. It was a tremendous struggle, both physically and emotionally. The time away from him was filled with a great deal of anxiety and sadness. In contrast, being able to breastfeed him once I got home seemed to bring both of us great comfort and instant connection. Being a breastfeeding mother who works out of the home was more work than I could have imagined. However, I plan to do it all over again with our second child who is due any day now, because it was totally worth it.

Appendix A

For the Caregiver of a Breastfed Baby

You already know that you make a difference to the breastfed baby in your care. But you may not know what a key role you play in helping the baby's mother meet her breastfeeding goals. Here are some of the ways you can support her.

Avoid Overfeeding

If the baby takes too much milk while the mother is away, the baby will be less interested in breastfeeding when they are together. Less breastfeeding puts the mother's milk supply at risk. She may also need to provide more pumped milk. Anything you can do to reduce the amount of milk the mother needs to pump makes her life easier. Here are more basics.

Know breastfeeding norms. Most breastfed babies take smaller feedings and feed more often than babies fed formula. At an average feeding, a breastfed baby older than 1 month takes 3 to 4 oz. (90 to 120 mL) of milk.

Feed when the baby shows signs of hunger, rather than on a schedule. Cues such as rooting and hand-to-mouth mean it's time to feed. It is common for breastfed babies to feed more often during some parts of the day than others.

Feed slowly using paced bottle feeding. When fed slowly, the baby feels full with less milk, reducing the mother's need to pump. If the baby is older than 6 to 7 months, she may be fed by cup. If bottle fed, expect feedings to take about 15 to 30 minutes. Here's how paced bottle feeding works:

Hold the baby semi-upright or upright and tap her lips with the nipple until she opens wide.

- Help the baby latch far enough onto the nipple so her lips close on the nipple's base rather than its shaft or tip. (Gagging means baby needs a shorter nipple.) If the baby's lips are pulled in, use your fingers to flange them out.

- During feedings, hold the bottle nearly horizontal, so the flow isn't too fast.

- Build in pauses every few minutes by lowering the end of the bottle so milk runs out of the nipple. Or remove the nipple from the baby's mouth and rest it on her lower lip.

- Repeat throughout the feeding until the baby is done. Switch sides halfway through.

- Stop when the baby stops, even if there's milk left.

- Burp the baby after feeding to bring up any air.

Watch a demonstration of paced bottle feeding in this video: *http://www.youtube.com/watch?v=UH4T7OOSzGs&feature=youtu.be*

Encourage Breastfeeding

One key way the mother keeps her milk production steady is frequent breastfeeding. You can help by encouraging her to sit down and breastfeed just before leaving the baby with you and as soon as she returns. To make this easier:

- Make comfortable seating available.

- Offer a private area for nursing, if desired.

- Make it clear that breastfeeding is welcome and encouraged.

- If the mother is due to arrive soon and the baby seems hungry, feed just a little milk until she arrives to breastfeed.

The more times each day a mother breastfeeds, the less milk she must pump. Breastfed babies need, on average, about 25 to 30 oz. (750 to 900 mL) per day. The more milk the baby gets directly from mother, the less pumped milk is needed.

Store and Handle Milk with Care

You can also support the mother by handling her milk with care so that little milk is discarded.

- Let the mother know if the baby regularly takes less milk than is in her containers.

- Follow the milk storage guidelines she provides.

- Thaw and warm milk gently and gradually, keeping heat low. Swirl the milk to mix it. Don't shake it.

Milk can be thawed in the refrigerator overnight. You can also thaw or warm milk in other ways.

- Hold the container under warm running water for a few minutes.

- Hold the container in water previously heated on the stove. Do not heat the milk directly on the burner.

If you use water to thaw or warm milk, tilt or hold the container, so that the water cannot seep under the lid. Feed thawed milk right away or refrigerate it.

Do not thaw or warm milk in a microwave, which changes the milk and heats it unevenly. Even if you swirl (or even shake) the milk afterwards, hot spots remain that can burn the baby's throat.

By supporting breastfeeding in these ways, you can provide great quality of care for the breastfed baby. At the same time, you can make life easier for the mother and her entire family.

You can download a copy of this handout at: *http://issuu.com/nancymohrbacher/docs/caregiverbfbaby*

Milk Storage Guidelines for Healthy, Full-Term Babies at Home

Tempurature	Deep Freezer (0°F/-18°C)	Refrigerator Freezer (variable) (0°F/ -18°C)	Refrigerator (39°F/4°C)	Insulated Cooler with Ice Packs (59°F/15°C)	Room Temperature (66°F-72°F/ 19°C-22°C)	(73°F-77°F / 23°C-25°C)
Fresh	Ideal: 6 mos. Okay: 12 mos.	3-4 mos.	Ideal: 72 hrs. Okay: 8 days	24 hrs.	6-10 hrs.	4 hrs.
Frozen Thawed in Fridge	Do not refreeze	Do not refreeze	24 hrs.	Do not Store	4 hrs.	4hrs.
Thawed, Warmed, Not Fed	Do not refreeze	Do not refreeze	4 hrs.	Do not Store	Until feeding ends	Until feeding ends
Warmed, Fed	Discard	Discard	Discard	Discard	Until Feeding ends	Until feeding ends

Appendix B

How to Hand Express Milk

Hand expression can be a useful way to relieve breast fullness, boost milk production, and provide milk for your baby. Here's how to do it.

Getting ready

First, wash your hands well. Find a clean collection container with a wide mouth, like a cup. If possible, express in a private, comfortable place where you can relax. Feeling relaxed enhances milk flow.

Find your sweet spot

Whichever hand-expression technique you use, the key is finding your "sweet spot," the area on your breast where milk flows fastest when it is compressed. Try different finger positions until you find it. If the dark area around your nipple (areola) is large, your sweet spot may be inside it. If it is small, your sweet spot may be outside it.

Do what works best and expresses the most milk

This method combines the World Health Organization technique with others:

1. Before expressing, gently massage your breasts with your hands and fingertips or a soft baby brush or warm towel.

2. Sit up and lean slightly forward, so gravity helps milk flow.

3. To find your sweet spot, start with your thumb on top of the breast and fingers below, both about 1.5 inches (4 cm) from the base of the nipple. Some mothers find it helpful to curl their hand and use just the tips of their fingers and thumb. Apply steady pressure several times into the breast toward the chest wall. If no milk comes, shift finger and thumb either closer to or farther from the nipple and compress again a few times. Repeat, moving finger and thumb until you feel slightly firmer breast tissue and gentle pressure yields milk. After finding your sweet spot, skip the "finding" phase and start with your fingers on this area.

4. Apply steady pressure on areas of milk in the breast by pressing fingers toward the chest wall, not toward the nipple.

5. While applying inward pressure on the breast, compress thumb and finger pads together (pushing in, not pulling out toward the nipple). Find a good rhythm of press—compress—relax, like a baby's suckling rhythm.

6. Switch breasts every few minutes (5 or 6 times in total at each expression) while rotating finger position around the breast. After expressing, all areas of the breast should feel soft. This process usually takes about 20 to 30 minutes.

If needed, adjust

Hand expression should feel comfortable. If not, you may be compressing too hard, sliding your fingers along the skin, or squeezing the nipple. If you feel discomfort, review the instructions, and adjust your technique. It is important to find the method that works best for you. You can find several demonstration videos online by doing a search for "hand expression of breast milk."

Sample Plans for Different Work Schedules

There are many ways to plan your day. The following sample plans are intended to give you some ideas to try or to suggest to your employer. Ultimately, as always, do what works best for you.

Full-Time Job

A full-time job may consist of the traditional eight-hour day, five days per week. But it may not. Some women work much longer days, so samples of both are shown here. These schedules should work well for women with a small to medium breast storage capacity. If you have a large storage capacity, you may be able to pump fewer times during your work day without a dip in your milk production.

Eight-Hour Workdays

Traditional 8 a.m. to 5 p.m. work day, small-to-medium storage capacity

5:30 a.m.: Wake, nurse baby (dream feed), get ready for the day.

7:15 a.m.: Breastfeed baby at childcare provider before leaving for work.

8:00 a.m.: Arrive at work.

10:00-10:25 a.m.: Pump (with a drink and/or snack).

12:00-1:00 p.m.: Lunch break, pump or breastfeed while eating.

3:00-3:25 p.m.: Pump (with a drink and/or snack).

5:00 p.m.: Leave work.

5:20 p.m.: Breastfeed at caregiver before leaving for home.

At home: Encourage frequent feedings.

Job with afternoon/evening shift, small-to-medium storage capacity

During the morning: Encourage frequent feedings.

12:15 p.m.: Feed baby at childcare provider right before leaving for work.

1:00 p.m.: Arrive at work.

3:00-3:25 p.m.: Pump break (with a drink and/or snack).

6:00-6:30 p.m.: Meal break, pump or breastfeed while eating.

8:30-8:55 p.m.: Pump break (with a drink and/or snack).

10:00 p.m.: Leave work.

10:20 p.m.: Do a dream feed with baby at childcare provider before leaving for home.

At home: Encourage frequent feedings.

12-Hour Workdays

Day job, small-to-medium storage capacity

5:30 a.m.: Wake, nurse baby (dream feed), get ready for the day.

7:15 a.m.: Breastfeed baby at childcare provider before leaving for work.

8:00 a.m.: Arrive at work.

10:00-10:25 a.m.: Pump (with a drink and/or snack).

12:00-1:00 p.m.: Lunch break, pump or breastfeed while eating.

3:00-3:25 p.m.: Pump (with a drink and/or snack).

6:00-6:30 p.m.: Dinner break, pump or breastfeed while eating.

8:00 p.m.: Leave for childcare provider.

8:30 p.m.: Breastfeed at caregiver before leaving for home.

At home: Encourage frequent feedings.

Part-Time Job

Your need to pump will vary, depending on your job schedule. For example, if you'll be working three days per week, milk production may be easier to manage if you alternate days at work with days at home. That way, if your daily total dips one day, your baby can nurse like crazy the next day so that it rebounds. Choose a schedule that works best for you. Here are some possibilities.

Several Long Days

See the eight-hour and 12-hour sample schedules in the previous section as a starting point. If you have a large breast storage capacity or you are alternating work days, you may be able to keep your milk stable with fewer pump sessions per day.

Many Short Days

To pump or not to pump, that is the question. The length of your work day and your breast storage capacity will determine the best plan for you. If your work day is no longer than the longest stretch between feedings at home, then pumping at work is optional. If you want to store milk for work days, you can pump after feedings at home. Here's an example. Swati returned to work as a barrista in a coffee shop when her baby, Taj, was 8 weeks old. She was scheduled for five six-hour shifts per week, from 12 to 6 p.m. During her maternity leave, Taj had begun sleeping for six-hour stretches at night. When he woke to feed, Swati felt full but not uncomfortable. Taj took a 4 oz. (160 mL) bottle while she was at work. To store milk for her baby, rather than pumping in the middle of her work shift, Swati decided to pump once every morning about an hour after her first feeding and again after work after she nursed Taj. During those pump sessions, she was able to store enough milk for the one feeding her baby took during work.

But going for six-hour stretches without pumping or breastfeeding wouldn't be the best option for every mother. Here's another example. Breastfeeding was going well for Hiroko and her baby Sen. Hiroko returned to work as a server in a catering business when Sen was 12 weeks old. She worked evenings at events, and her shifts were six hours long. During his first three months, Sen had never gone longer than four hours between feedings and when he did, Hiroko felt full-to-bursting. Hiroko arranged to take pumping breaks midway in her shift, at about the three-hour mark, at which she pumped enough for her baby's feeding on her next work day.

Resources

Finding Skilled Breastfeeding Help

If you're in need of breastfeeding help, don't wait to find someone. Usually, the sooner you get help, the easier it is to solve your problem. When contacting local breast-feeding specialists, be aware that different credentials reflect different levels of education and training. A variety of initials (CLC, CLE, CBE, CBC, LE, and others) are awarded after attending a brief training course, usually less than one week long. A person with these initials may be able to provide some help but may have limited skills, understanding, and experience.

The credential IBCLC, however, indicates—at the least—a basic competence in the field of lactation. These initials stand for "International Board Certified Lactation Consultant." To receive this credential, a person must pass an all-day certifying exam. To qualify to take that exam, she must first have a combination of formal education, breast-feeding education, and thousands of hours working one-on-one with breastfeeding mothers and babies. There are several ways you can find a local IBCLC.

- Click on the "Find a Lactation Consultant" link on *www.ilca.org* and enter your ZIP or postal code. ILCA is the International Lactation Consultant Association, the professional association for lactation consultants. Not all international board certified lactation consultants are members.

- Contact your local birthing facility and ask to speak to the breastfeeding specialist. Ask if she can help you or if she knows someone in your community who can.

- Contact your local public-health department and ask if there is any IBCLCs on staff who can help you.

- Contact mother-to-mother breastfeeding support people in your area (see next section) and ask them for suggestions. They may know the best choices in your area.

Another possible source of skilled breastfeeding help is the mother-to-mother support organizations listed in the next section. These experienced breastfeeding mothers work as volunteers to help other mothers. Their skill level can run the gamut from highly skilled to inexperienced. Hopefully, if they can't help you, they'll know someone who can.

Getting the Support You Need

Don't underestimate the importance of ongoing breast-feeding support. What's really great today is that breast-feeding support comes in many forms. Even if you are in a remote location, work odd hours, or lack safe, reliable transportation, you can access the many Facebook groups and online forums that support employed breastfeeding mothers. To get a sense of what's out there and its immense value, see Lara Audelo's book, *The Virtual Breastfeeding Culture: Seeking Mother-to-Mother Support in the Digital Age.*

Mother-to-Mother Breastfeeding Organizations

It's always a plus to have choices, and sometimes there's just no substitute for spending face time with other mothers and babies. Mother-to-mother breastfeeding organizations that offer in-person meetings (as well as online and Facebook support options) are:

- Breastfeeding USA (*www.breastfeedingusa.org*), this rapidly growing nonprofit organization was formed in 2010 with a focus on providing evidence-based information and support in a variety of formats.

- Australian Breastfeeding Association (*www.breastfeeding.asn.au*). This long-standing beacon of breastfeeding support offers a range of services, such as classes, email counseling, a 24-hour Breastfeeding Helpline, online forums, and local support groups.

In the U.K., there are several national breastfeeding support organizations. A list of their links is at: *http:// www.nhs.uk/Conditions/pregnancy-and-baby/pages/breastfeeding-help-support.aspx# close*

Another mother-to-mother option in most countries is La Leche League International (*www.llli.org*), the grandmother of breastfeeding support, which has been helping mothers since 1956 and offers in-person meetings, phone, and email help. One way La Leche League differs from other breastfeeding organizations is that it requires its leaders to follow its parenting philosophy, which is consistent with attachment parenting. It does not require those who seek help from La Leche League to follow its philosophy.

Doulas

"Doula" comes from the Greek word for servant, and refers to someone who provides practical and emotional help to women before, during, and after birth. Many doulas also offer breastfeeding help and support.

- DONA International (*www.dona.org*) lists labor-support and postpartum doulas.

- Find a Doula, Australia (*http://www.findadoula.com.au/*) to locale doulas in Australia.

- Doula U.K. (*http://doula.org.uk/*) to locate labor and postpartum/postnatal doulas.

Websites

The internet can be an unreliable place. All breastfeeding websites are definitely not created equal! Here are some that you can trust.

- *Kellymom.com* is a great site that includes articles on almost every aspect of breastfeeding.

- *NancyMohrbacher.com* includes a section for employed breastfeeding mothers and many articles on hot topics.

- *BreastfeedingMadeSimple.com* is the companion site for the book I co-authored with Kathleen Kendall-Tackett, *Breastfeeding Made Simple.* It has many resources for a wide range of breastfeeding concerns and common challenges.

- *WomensHealth.gov/breastfeeding/government-in-action/business-case.html* Here you can download *The Business Case for Breastfeeding,* which includes materials for mothers, human resources, CEOs, etc. A treasure trove of great resources.

- *Womenshealth.gov/breastfeeding/employer-solutions/index.php* A new U.S. Government website for working and breastfeeding mothers and their employers.

- *BestforBabes.org* offers resources for employed mothers, as well as ways to avoid "booby traps."

- *BreastfeedingPartners.org*. Click on the "Work & School" tab to find its *Making It Work Toolkit,* a great resource.

- *Workandpump.com*. This site is an oldie but a goodie that is chock full of great info.

- *BreastfeedingUSA.org* offers many helpful articles and a locator for local support.

- *Breastfeedinginc.ca* has many helpful articles and videos by Canadian pediatrician and lactation consultant, Dr. Jack Newman.

- *Isisonline.org.uk* offers evidence-based information for parents and professionals about infant sleep norms.

- *Lowmilksupply.org* was created by two lactation consultants who specialize in milk production issues.

Free Online Videos

Hand Expression: *http://newborns.stanford.edu/Breastfeeding/HandExpression.html*

Hands-on Pumping: *http://newborns.stanford.edu/Breastfeeding/MaxProduction.html*

Paced Bottle Feeding for the Breastfed Baby: *http://www.youtube.com/watch?v=UH4T70OSzGs&feature=youtube*

Reverse Pressure Softening. How to Relieve Engorgement: *http://www.youtube.com/watch?v=2_RD9HN-rOJ8&oref=http%3A%2F%2Fwww.youtube.com%2F-watch%3Fv%3D2_RD9HNrOJ8&has_verified=1*

Books

These resources would be great additions to any employed mother's bookshelf.

Audelo, L. (2013). *The virtual breastfeeding culture: Seeking mother-to-mother support in the digital age.* Amarillo, TX Praeclarus Press.

Mohrbacher, N., & Kendall-Tackett, K. (2010). *Breastfeeding made simple: Seven natural laws for nursing mothers, 2nd Ed.* Oakland, CA: New Harbinger Publications.

Mohrbacher, N. (2013). *Breastfeeding solutions: Quick tips for the most common nursing challenges.* Oakland, CA: New Harbinger Publications.

Peterson, A., & Harmer, M. (2010). *Balancing breast and bottle: Reaching your breastfeeding goals.* Amarillo, TX: Hale Publishing.

Rapley, G., & Murkett, T. (2010). *Baby-led weaning: The essential guide to introducing solid foods–and helping your baby to grow up a happy and confident eater.* New York: The Experiment.

Roche-Paull, R. (2010). *Breastfeeding in combat boots: A survival guide to successful breastfeeding while serving in the military.* Amarillo, TX: Hale Publishing.

West, D., & Marasco, L. (2009). *The breastfeeding mothers' guide to making more milk.* New York: McGraw-Hill.

Smartphone App

Here's a basic breastfeeding resource you can download to your Android or iPhone. It covers the 30 most common breastfeeding challenges, and includes the milk-storage guidelines in this book. Use your smartphone to open this link and you're on your way.

Breastfeeding Solutions by Nancy Mohrbacher. (2013). Available for Android and iPhones from Amazon, Google Play, and the App Store.

http://www.nancymohrbacher.com/app-support/

Breast Pumps to Buy or Rent

Here is the contact information for the three recommended breast-pump brands.

Ameda Breast Pumps

To locate an Ameda rental pump or purchase an Ameda Purely Yours pump near you, call Ameda Breastfeeding Products, at 1-866-99AMEDA (1-866-992-6332), or go online to *www.Ameda.com*.

Hygeia Breast Pumps

To locate a Hygeia rental pump or a Hygeia Enjoye purchase pump near you, call Hygeia at 1-888-786-7466 or go online to *www.Hygeiainc.com*.

Medela Breast Pumps

To locate a Medela rental pump or purchase a Medela Pump In Style or Freestyle pump near you, contact Medela, Inc., at 1-800-TELLYOU (in the U.S.) or go online to *www. medela.com*.

Other Products

Hands-Free Pumping Devices

For the latest commercial products that help you pump hands-free, just Google "hands-free pumping." Some women make their own. Here are two options:

- This free tutorial uses elastic hair bands: *http://kelly-mom.com/bf/pumpingmoms/pumping/hands-free-pumping/*

- This one (be sure to click on the pictures) uses rubber bands: *http://www.workandpump.com/handsfree.htm*

Prevent Milk Leakage

To find LilyPadz, the silicone product that applies pressure to the nipples to prevent milk leakage, go online to *www.lilypadz.com*.

Collect Leaked Milk

To find Milkies milk savers, the container you wear to collect milk while your baby breastfeeds, go online to *http://www.mymilkies.com/milksaver*.

References

American Academy of Pediatrics (AAP). (2012). Breast-feeding and the use of human milk. *Pediatrics, 129*(3), e827-e841.

American Academy of Pediatrics. (AAP). (2011). SIDS and other sleep-related infant deaths: expansion of recommendations for a safe infant sleeping environment. *Pediatrics, 128*(5), 1030-1039.

American Academy of Pediatrics. (AAP). (2001). The use and misuse of fruit juice in pediatrics. *Pediatrics, 107*(5), 1210-1213.

Blyton, D. M., Sullivan, C. E., & Edwards, N. (2002). Lactation is associated with an increase in slow-wave sleep in women. *Journal of Sleep Research, 11*(4), 297-303.

Boushey, H., & Glynn, S. J. (2012). There are significant business costs to replacing employees. Retrieved from: *http://www.americanprogress.org/wp-content/uploads/2012/11/CostofTurnover.pdf*

Brusseau, R. (1998). *Bacterial analysis of refrigerated human milk following infant feeding.* Unpublished senior thesis. Concordia University.

Centers for Disease Control and Prevention. (CDC). (2013). Unmarried childbearing. Retrieved from: *http://www.cdc.gov/nchs/fastats/unmarry.htm*

Centers for Disease Control and Prevention. (CDC). (2012). Percentage of breastfed U.S. children who are supplemented with infant formula, by birth year. Retrieved from *http://www.cdc.gov/breastfeeding/data/nis_data/*

Chatterji, P., & Markowitz, S. (2012). Family leave after childbirth and the mental health of new mothers. *The Journal of Mental Health Policy and Economics, 15*(2), 61-76.

Cohen, R., Lange, L., & Slusser, W. (2002). A description of a male-focused breastfeeding promotion corporate lactation program. *Journal of Human Lactation, 18*(1), 61-65.

Cohen, R., & Mrtek, M. B. (1994). The impact of two corporate lactation programs on the incidence and duration of breast-feeding by employed mothers. *American Journal of Health Promotion, 8*(6), 436-441.

Cohen, R., Mrtek, M. B., & Mrtek, R. G. (1995). Comparison of maternal absenteeism and infant illness rates among breast-feeding and formula-feeding women in two corporations. *American Journal of Health Promotion, 10*(2), 148-153.

Colson, S. D., Meek, J. H., & Hawdon, J. M. (2008). Optimal positions for the release of primitive neonatal reflexes stimulating breastfeeding. *Early Human Development, 84*(7), 441-449.

DaMota, K., Banuelos, J., Goldbronn, J., Vera-Beccera, L. E., & Heinig, M. J. (2012). Maternal request for in-hospital supplementation of healthy breastfed infants among low-income women. *Journal of Human Lactation, 28*(4), 476-482.

Dewey, K. G., & Brown, K. H. (2003). Update on technical issues concerning complementary feeding of young children in developing countries and implications for intervention programs. *Food and Nutrition Bulletin, 24*(1), 5-28.

Doan, T., Gardiner, A., Gay, C. L., & Lee, K. A. (2007). Breast-feeding increases sleep duration of new parents. *Journal of Perinatal and Neonatal Nursing, 21*(3), 200-206.

Dunn, B. F., Zavela, K. J., Cline, A. D., & Cost, P. A. (2004). Breastfeeding practices in Colorado businesses. *Journal of Human Lactation, 20*(2), 170-177.

Geddes, D. T. (2009). The use of ultrasound to identify milk ejection in women: Tips and pitfalls. *International Breast-feeding Journal, 4*, 5.

Goldblum, R. M., Garza, C., Johnson, C. A., Harrist, R., & Nichols, B. L. (1981). Human milk banking I: Effects of container upon immunologic factors in mature milk. *Nutrition Research, 1*, 449-459.

Hale, T. W. (2012). *Medications & Mothers' Milk* (15th Ed.). Amarillo, TX: Hale Publishing.

Hammond, K. A. (1997). Adaptation of the maternal intestine during lactation. *Journal of Mammary Gland Biology and Neoplasia, 2*(3), 243-252.

Heinig, M. J., Nommsen, L. A., Peerson, J. M., Lonnerdal, B., & Dewey, K. G. (1993). Energy and protein intakes of breast-fed and formula-fed infants during the first year of life and their association with growth velocity: The DARLING Study. *American Journal of Clinical Nutrition, 58*(2), 152-161.

Hennart, P., Delogne-Desnoeck, J., Vis, H., & Robyn, C. (1981). Serum levels of prolactin and milk production in women during a lactation period of thirty months. *Clinical Endocrinology (Oxf), 14*(4), 349-353.

Hicks, J. B. (Ed.). (2006). *Hirkani's daughters: Women who scale modern mountains to combine breastfeeding and working*. Schaumburg, IL: La Leche League International.

Hill, P. D., Aldag, J. C., Chatterton, R. T., & Zinaman, M. (2005). Comparison of milk output between mothers of preterm and term infants: The first 6 weeks after birth. *Journal of Human Lactation, 21*(1), 22-30.

HRSA. (2008). *The business case for breastfeeding*. Retrieved from: *http://www.womenshealth.gov/breastfeeding/government-in-action/business-case-for-breastfeeding/*.

Islam, M. M., Peerson, J. M., Ahmed, T., Dewey, K. G., & Brown, K. H. (2006). Effects of varied energy density of complementary foods on breast-milk intakes and total energy consumption by healthy, breastfed Bangladeshi children. *American Journal of Clinical Nutrition, 83*(4), 851-858.

Jones, E., & Hilton, S. (2009). Correctly fitting breast shields are the key to lactation success for pump dependent mothers following preterm delivery. *Journal of Neonatal Nursing, 15*(1), 14-17.

Jones, F., & Tully, M. R. (2011). *Best practices for expressing, storing and handling human milk* (3rd Ed.). Raleigh, NC: Human Milk Banking Association of North America.

Kearney, M. H., & Cronenwett, L. (1991). Breastfeeding and employment. *Journal of Obstetric, Gynecologic & Neonatal Nursing, 20*(6), 471-480.

Kendall-Tackett, K., Cong, Z., & Hale, T. W. (2011). The effect of feeding method on sleep duration, maternal well-being, and postpartum depression. *Clinical Lactation, 2*(2), 22-26.

Kent, J. C. (2007). How breastfeeding works. *Journal of Midwifery & Women's Health, 52*(6), 564-570.

Kent, J. C., Hepworth, A. R., Sherriff, J. L., Cox, D. B., Mitoulas, L. R., & Hartmann, P. E. (2013). Longitudinal changes in breastfeeding patterns from 1 to 6 months of lactation. *Breastfeeding Medicine, 8*, 401-407.

Kent, J. C., Mitoulas, L., Cox, D. B., Owens, R. A., & Hartmann, P. E. (1999). Breast volume and milk production during extended lactation in women. *Experimental Physiology, 84*(2), 435-447.

Kent, J. C., Mitoulas, L. R., Cregan, M. D., Geddes, D. T., Larsson, M., Doherty, D. A., et al. (2008). Importance of vacuum for breast milk expression. *Breastfeeding Medicine, 3*(1), 11-19.

Kent, J. C., Mitoulas, L. R., Cregan, M. D., Ramsay, D. T., Doherty, D. A., & Hartmann, P. E. (2006). Volume and frequency of breastfeedings and fat content of breast milk throughout the day. *Pediatrics, 117*(3), e387-395.

Kent, J. C., Prime, D. K., & Garbin, C. P. (2011). Principles for maintaining or increasing breast milk production. *Journal of Obstetric, Gynecologic, & Neonatal Nursing.* doi: 10.1111/j.1552-6909.2011.01313.x.

Kent, J. C., Ramsay, D. T., Doherty, D., Larsson, M., & Hartmann, P. E. (2003). Response of breasts to different stimulation patterns of an electric breast pump. *Journal of Human Lactation, 19*(2), 179-186.

Kimbro, R. T. (2006). On-the-job moms: Work and breastfeeding initiation and duration for a sample of low-income women. *Maternal & Child Health Journal, 10*(1), 19-26.

Kline, T. S., & Lash, S. R. (1964). The bleeding nipple of pregnancy and postpartum period: A cytologic and histologic study. *Acta Cytologica, 8,* 336-340.

Kramer, M. S., Guo, T., Platt, R. W., Vanilovich, I., Sevkovskaya, Z., Dzikovich, I., et al. (2004). Feeding effects on growth during infancy. *Journal of Pediatrics, 145*(5), 600-605.

Kramer, M. S., & Kakuma, R. (2012). Optimal duration of exclusive breastfeeding. *Cochrane Database of Systematic Reviews, Art No. CD003517.*

La Leche League International. (LLLI). (2008). *Storing human milk.* Schaumburg, IL: Author.

Lawrence, R. A., & Lawrence, R. M. (2011). *Breastfeeding: A guide for the medical profession* (7th Ed.). Philadelphia, PA: Elsevier Mosby.

Li, R., Fein, S. B., & Grummer-Strawn, L. M. (2008). Association of breastfeeding intensity and bottle-emptying behaviors at early infancy with infants' risk for excess weight at late infancy. *Pediatrics, 122* (Suppl 2), S77-84.

Li, R., Magadia, J., Fein, S. B., & Grummer-Strawn, L. M. (2012). Risk of bottle-feeding for rapid weight gain during the first year of life. *Archives of Pediatric & Adolescent Medicine, 166*(5), 431-436.

Macknin, M. L., Medendorp, S. V., & Maier, M. C. (1989). Infant sleep and bedtime cereal. *American Journal of Diseases of Children, 143*(9), 1066-1068.

Manohar, A. A., Williamson, M., & Koppikar, G. V. (1997). Effect of storage of colostrum in various containers. *Indian Pediatrics, 34*(4), 293-295.

McGovern, P., Dowd, B., Gjerdingen, D., Dagher, R., Ukestad, L., McCaffrey, D., et al. (2007). Mothers' health and work-related factors at 11 weeks postpartum. *The Annals of Family Medicine, 5*(6), 519-527.

McGovern, P., Dowd, B., Gjerdingen, D., Gross, C. R., Kenney, S., Ukestad, L., et al. (2006). Postpartum health of employed mothers 5 weeks after childbirth. *Annals of Family Medicine, 4*(2), 159-167.

McKenna, J. J., & McDade, T. (2005). Why babies should never sleep alone: A review of the co-sleeping controversy in relation to SIDS, bedsharing and breast feeding. *Paediatric Respiratory Reviews, 6*(2), 134-152.

Meier, P. (1988). Bottle- and breast-feeding: Effects on transcutaneous oxygen pressure and temperature in preterm infants. *Nursing Research, 37*(1), 36-41.

Meier, P., & Anderson, G. C. (1987). Responses of small preterm infants to bottle- and breast-feeding. *MCN American Journal of Maternal Child Nursing, 12*(2), 97-105.

Meier, P., Motykowski, J. E., & Zuleger, J. L. (2004). Choosing a correctly-fitted breast shield for milk expression. *Medela Messenger, 21*, 8-9.

Mohrbacher, N. (2011). The magic number and long-term milk production. *Clinical Lactation, 2*(1), 15-18.

Mohrbacher, N. (2010). *Breastfeeding answers made simple.* Amarillo, TX: Hale Publishing.

Molbak, K., Gottschau, A., Aaby, P., Hojlyng, N., Ingholt, L., & da Silva, A. P. (1994). Prolonged breast feeding, diarrhoeal disease, and survival of children in Guinea-Bissau. *British Medical Journal, 308*(6941), 1403-1406.

Morton, J., Hall, J. Y., Wong, R. J., Thairu, L., Benitz, W. E., & Rhine, W. D. (2009). Combining hand techniques with electric pumping increases milk production in mothers of preterm infants. *Journal of Perinatology, 29*(11), 757-764.

Morton, J., Wong, R. J., Hall, J. Y., Pang, W. W., Lai, C. T., Lui, J., et al. (2012). Combining hand techniques with electric pumping increases the caloric content of milk in mothers of preterm infants. *Journal of Perinatology, 32*(10), 791-796.

Neville, M. C., Allen, J. C., Archer, P. C., Casey, C. E., Seacat, J., Keller, R. P., et al. (1991). Studies in human lactation: milk volume and nutrient composition during weaning and lactogenesis. *American Journal of Clinical Nutrition, 54*(1), 81-92.

Nichols, M. R., & Roux, G. M. (2004). Maternal perspectives on postpartum return to the workplace. *Journal of Obstetric, Gynecologic, & Neonatal Nursing, 33*(4), 463-471.

Nielsen, S. B., Reilly, J. J., Fewtrell, M. S., Eaton, S., Grinham, J., & Wells, J. C. (2011). Adequacy of milk intake during exclusive breastfeeding: A longitudinal study. *Pediatrics, 128*(4), e907-914.

NWLC. (2012). *The next generation of Title IX: Pregnant and parenting students* [Electronic Version]. Retrieved from: *http://www.titleix.info/history/history-overview.aspx*

Odom, E. C., Li, R., Scanlon, K. S., Perrine, C. G., & Grummer-Strawn, L. (2013). Reasons for earlier than desired cessation of breastfeeding. *Pediatrics, 131*(3), e726-732.

OECD. (2011). Health at a glance 2011: OECD Indicators: 4.9 Caesarean sections. Retrieved from: *http://www.oecd-ilibrary.org/sites/health_glance-2011-en/04/09/g4-09-01.html?itemId=/content/chapter/health_glance-2011-37-en*

Ogbuanu, C., Glover, S., Probst, J., Hussey, J., & Liu, J. (2011). Balancing work and family: Effect of employment characteristics on breastfeeding. *Journal of Human Lactation, 27*(3), 225-238.

Ogbuanu, C., Glover, S., Probst, J., Liu, J., & Hussey, J. (2011). The effect of maternity leave length and time of return to work on breastfeeding. *Pediatrics, 127*(6), e1414-1427.

Ortiz, J., McGilligan, K., & Kelly, P. (2004). Duration of breast milk expression among working mothers enrolled in an employer-sponsored lactation program. *Pediatric Nursing, 30*(2), 111-119.

PAHO/WHO. (2001). Guiding principles for complementary feeding of the breastfed child. Retrieved from: *http://whqlibdoc.who.int/paho/2004/a85622.pdf*.

Paxson, C. L., Jr., & Cress, C. C. (1979). Survival of human milk leukocytes. *Journal of Pediatrics, 94*(1), 61-64.

Perrine, C. G., Scanlon, K. S., Li, R., Odom, E., & Grummer-Strawn, L. M. (2012). Baby-Friendly hospital practices and meeting exclusive breastfeeding intention. *Pediatrics, 130*(1), 54-60.

Peterson, A., & Harmer, M. (2010). *Balancing breast & bottle: Reaching your breastfeeding goals.* Amarillo, TX: Hale Publishing.

Pittard, W. B., 3rd, & Bill, K. (1981). Human milk banking. Effect of refrigeration on cellular components. *Clinical Pediatrics, 20*(1), 31-33.

Prime, D. K., Kent, J. C., Hepworth, A. R., Trengove, N. J., & Hartmann, P. E. (2012). Dynamics of milk removal during simultaneous breast expression in women. *Breastfeeding Medicine, 7*(2), 100-106.

Quan, R., Yang, C., Rubinstein, S., Lewiston, N. J., Sunshine, P., Stevenson, D. K., et al. (1992). Effects of microwave radiation on anti-infective factors in human milk. *Pediatrics, 89*(4 Pt 1), 667-669.

Rechtman, D. J., Lee, M. L., & Berg, H. (2006). Effect of environmental conditions on unpasteurized donor human milk. *Breastfeeding Medicine, 1*(1), 24-26.

Roe, B., Whittington, L. A., Fein, S. B., & Teisl, M. F. (1999). Is there competition between breast-feeding and maternal employment? *Demography, 36*(2), 157-171.

SHRM. (2013). *2012 employee benefits research report.* Retrieved from: *http://www.shrm.org/research/surveyfindings/articles/pages/2012employeebenefitsresearchreport.aspx*

Sievers, E., Oldigs, H. D., Santer, R., & Schaub, J. (2002). Feeding patterns in breast-fed and formula-fed infants. *Annals of Nutrition and Metabolism, 46*(6), 243-248.

Skafida, V. (2012). Juggling work and motherhood: The impact of employment and maternity leave on breast-feeding duration: A survival analysis on Growing Up in Scotland data. *Maternal and Child Health Journal, 16*(2), 519-527.

Slusser, W. M., Lange, L., Dickson, V., Hawkes, C., & Cohen, R. (2004). Breast milk expression in the workplace: A look at frequency and time. *Journal of Human Lactation, 20*(2), 164-169.

Stuebe, A. M., & Rich-Edwards, J. W. (2009). The reset hypothesis: Lactation and maternal metabolism. *American Journal of Perinatology, 26*(1), 81-88.

Stuebe, A. M., Rich-Edwards, J. W., Willett, W. C., Manson, J. E., & Michels, K. B. (2005). Duration of lactation and incidence of type 2 diabetes. *Journal of the American Medical Association, 294*(20), 2601-2610.

Stuebe, A. M., & Schwarz, E. B. (2010). The risks and benefits of infant feeding practices for women and their children. *Journal of Perinatology, 30*(3), 155-162.

Takci, S., Gulmez, D., Yigit, S., Dogan, O., & Hascelik, G. (2013). Container type and bactericidal activity of human milk during refrigerated storage. *Journal of Human Lactation, 29*(3), 406-411.

Walker, M. (2011). *Breastfeeding and employment.* Amarillo, TX: Hale Publishing.

Walsh, W. (2011). *Single babe breastfeeding: It CAN be done!* Retrieved from: *http://www.bestforbabes.org/single-babe-breastfeeding-it-can-be-done*

Wang, W., Parker, K., & Taylor, P. (2013). *Breadwinner moms.* Washington, DC: Pew Research Center.

West, D., & Marasco, L. (2009). *The breastfeeding mother's guide to making more milk.* New York: McGraw Hill.

Williamson, M. T., & Murti, P. K. (1996). Effects of storage, time, temperature, and composition of containers on biologic components of human milk. *Journal of Human Lactation, 12*(1), 31-35.

Wilson-Clay, B., & Hoover, K. (2013). *The breastfeeding atlas* (5th Ed.). Manchaca, TX: LactNews Press.

World Health Organization. (WHO). (2010). Infant and young child feeding. Retrieved from: *http://www.who. int/mediacentre/factsheets/fs342/en/index.html*

Index

D

E

F

H

N

CPSIA information can be obtained
at www.ICGtesting.com
Printed in the USA
FSOW03n1302021115
12888FS